We hold these Truths to be Self Evident...
Where is the Self in Government?

By Rob Wright

Δ

Debates and party lines, protests and wars, rights given and taken away… it goes on and on. Our minds spin through the muck of a seemingly ailing country, world, and solar system stretching far beyond the view of our telescopes and satellites. A tired new voice emerges daily claiming this is the answer and that is not. The talking heads disagree or agree with said measures or persons, stirring the pot of debate over issues we did not even realize we faced while narrowing the scope of possible solution. Out-of-the-box thinking is successfully filtered.

Each opinion and its giver strive to prove they hold a monopoly on truth, and their side will be the key that unlocks a hidden utopia to finally bring the nation and world to a greater understanding. Citizens wait, either idly or frantically busying themselves for the arrival of the next politician or group to finally bring clarity to the unclear. Old issues are rehashed and new issues are drummed up in attempt to persuade an electorate that this will be the straw that breaks our back, and this will be the one thing that will fix it all.

This country has seen protests and debates ranging from war to civil rights for many years, but where has it brought us? Have we come closer to solving the issues; are the squeaky wheels finally receiving the grease? It seems, objectively, as the doomsday prognosticators with gnashing teeth circle the wagons, that we have only pushed each other away from the table of communion, a place where we can live and let live as a democratic republic, as a grand Constitution once promised, constructed during a time of greater uncertainty than our way of life had ever faced.

We have been through a time when we fought for freedoms, inalienable ones nonetheless. Freedoms allocated upon birthright by our Creator are now being negotiated by men in high places who are ruled by those who elected them, not by vote but by financial favor. They now decide which laws pertain to whom and who has the freedom to do what, both exactly and or vaguely.

Men and women who yearned for political, religious, and industrial freedom to pursue their own happiness tossed and turned, hoping to determine a plan which allowed such pursuit. Never did they precisely describe what happiness, religion, or industry was though they took deliberate steps to ensure we could all experience individual views of these.

For happiness, peace, and hope is derived of an individual experience. One man's happiness is another man's greatest fear. Those in fear scramble to regulate another's processes and foothold on happiness. There became that turning point where one neighbor, not finding happiness within their personal kingdom and path, sought to evaluate another neighbor's pursuit of a unique path toward a dream, finding it to be either startling, incomprehensible, or in contrast with their own set of values. When that focus shifted the neighbor began spending most of their time deconstructing and judging the other's path, causing the neighbor in question to feel the need to validate their very own journey.

In my youth, when civics was still taught in school, I learned a basic explanation of the aim and mission of democratic freedom. Quite simply, your freedom ends where another's begins. Straightforward, simple, succinct, however I wish to slightly amend such a concept. Our freedom ends nowhere essentially, for we are also free to respect the freedom of others. We are also free to set personal boundaries. It ends only upon such moment that we are injurious to another, and if we have became injurious we inherently injure our own freedom, and there are laws in place for these occurrences. The question we must ask ourselves in applying such reasonable thinking: What exactly is injurious to me? Certainly it is not all of the trivial trespasses to which we cry foul so frequently! We have started to place punitive worth on hurt feelings and petty disagreements, deeming them most injurious, negating the freedom to be strong in one's own standing, unyielding to the conceptions of others.

There exists no issue without two obvious sides and multitudes of other sides even yet to be perceived. There is spoken no statement without rebuttal among some portion of a body politic, even if that portion is a solitary individual. We can either continue the debate on what and who deserve what or how, or finally agree to disagree, without feeling like a debate inhibits our own pursuit of that magical yet undefined, individual paradigm of happiness. One does not have to be believed in order to pursue personal belief.

We have had teachers, pastors, gurus, clerics, rabbis, philosophers and so on deliver the message of self-evaluation and seeking, but somewhere we decided it prudent to evaluate our neighbor, telling them they are wrong and fight to keep our view the reigning status quo of the day or the era. In the meantime, we forget that government also has a "self", created by mirroring the very heart of its people, giving them the governing body they inevitably deserve.

That government, in turn, begins acting outside of its rightful duty, its Self, just as the people have. Without self-reflection it perpetuates a survival based policy structure, fearing that one day a group of barbarians, faceless and unnamed, will come to tear it out of our hands. There is a new villain for every new era whether it is personified as a group, nation, or social ill. This villain becomes the straw-man that we must ban together against, and when such villain loses its monstrous persona it fades, long before the war against it ends. We then change geography or public polling and create a new monster, for if there is nothing to fight, there is nothing to fear. If there is nothing to fear, we will feel safe, and if we feel safe, those in power feel powerless. A hero needs victims to protect, and men wishing to be heroes not birthed of altruism, but out of self importance and external validation become well intentioned villains who hide and plot in plain sight. They have perfected the art of making people believe that for freedom to exist we must fight and struggle to keep it, and help can only come from the powers that be, perpetuating a dynasty of fakers and hoaxers, preying on naivety of a people to maintain a stronghold on usefulness.

If we remain in the battlefield of the mind, we can always conjure a fear to defend against and a war to fight outside of ourselves; for it is far easier to destroy a city and control a region than it is to defeat the inner demons truly causing all of the trouble.

The same is true in our individual lives; we create faux monsters to fight in our nightmares and in our waking, hoping to prove we can still survive this cruel world and providing easy excuses as to why we fail. Yet the cruelty of this world has been completely concocted by a well constructed paradigm of fear that will only be dismantled through inward focus of the individual. The principle of failure has been perverted from that of being an inevitable outcome of trying various things before finally catching success, into a concept of finality and ultimately a validation of our fears and doubts.

It is time to heal, not fix, name-call, or vehemently swear we are right. We just need to heal, and the whole is healed by the same measure that heals the individual: internal seeking with compassion, love, and understanding, even when we admittedly do not fully understand. We do not have to understand how another person feels or believes. We observe it, yes, but it is up to them to understand themselves, and up to us to view differing opinions without getting our ego knotted up by something we oppose.

The answers for peace and cohabitation among a group of people as diverse as Americans had been provided for long ago and was bolstered by a Constitution derived from ancient philosophies of liberty and existence. It is we who think we lack the information and ability, and it is we who are buying into the greatest lie ever told—abundance must be fought for and procured, and happiness is only appropriate if *everyone* agrees that a particular way is the only true way, and all other ways inhibit the true way from evolving into fruition. This is the grand illusion, and too many are fighting in support of it no matter what party or creed from which they operate.

We have been taught of the great I AM, yet we run in the opposite direction from it, moment by moment. As soon as one owns "I am this…" as a concrete aspect of their being, they have gone too far, hoping to have found their validation of identity. You just are. Period. You are life in all of its vast diversity. Now be that completely, and let others be that as well, and we shall see how things turn out.

"I am conservative", "I am liberal", "I am libertarian", "I am straight", "I am gay", "I am a scientist", "I am a plumber", "I am Christian", "I am Buddhist", "I am Muslim", "I am Hindu", "I am American", "I am Chinese", "I am black", "I am white", "I am old", "I am young", "I am rich", "I am poor".

Dissecting these abrupt first-person proclamations, the only thing each one of these people has in common is "I AM". Every other tagline past those two words pigeonholes every debate and unique point of view. These two words that so perfectly and fully describe the state of consciousness are the only two that should bear any relevance mattering between another person's ears. It is time for us to find our own I AM, and dwell only in that space, caring not for another's tagline or classification of being, other than to honor and respect their personal quest and expression.

The mere ability to say and acknowledge *I AM* is the miracle of it all. If we do not stop to appreciate this miracle, such a simple, universal declarative then we, as a people, as a nation, and as a world are doomed.

If there is to be peace in the world,
There must be peace in the nations.

If there is to be peace in the nations,
There must be peace in the cities.

If there is to be peace in the cities,
There must be peace between neighbors.

If there is to be peace between neighbors,
There must be peace in the home.

If there is to be peace in the home,
There must be peace in the heart.

—Chinese philosopher - Lao-tse - 6th century BCE

The Illusion of Lack

Need and want, abundance and lack are intertwined in a foggy state of uncertainty, confusing generations, masking the true spirit of life. From birth, we are told to take care of our needs, before our wants. The "need" must be met to ensure happiness and stability. Yet as time goes on, embedding ourselves in overlapping human, mental creations of absolutes and presumed fears, we see a world constantly telling us to survive first, live second. Survive being hungry. Survive sickness and weather. Survive crime, taxes, wars and depressions... There is always something around the corner to prepare for! Something is always out to get us.

It seems silly and wrought with hyperbole; nonetheless, we have let it muddy our waters. How much of our day is spent planning for some scary, rainy day? This day is marked on an invisible calendar with invisible ink, approaching us as we hurl ourselves toward it, prepared or not. Hours, days, weeks, years lost, while perfectly peaceful moments are trampled by anxious preparation. "What if I lose my job? What if this doesn't work out? What if an asteroid hits the planet?"

What do we lack? For need automatically bases itself upon *not having*. Of course, as we spend our time on this planet, in this skin, there are certain things that are required such as clean air, food, water, etc. Even then, we can withstand those things for periods of time, and when we have witnessed previously that a life can change in one unpredicted instant, how urgently necessary is anything?

Setting sustenance, shelter, and air aside, we find there is little we would "need" for existence inasmuch to sustain us until the next golden moment. Our needs are intrinsically provided. The energy spent on worrying about what we seemingly need is wasted energy and perpetuates that state of thinking, in turn affecting perception, and your body's reaction to such.

Right out of the gate, we are teaching our children that a world of need exists, and they believe it more than they believe the Easter Bunny. It has become a subtle rule of life. We will need education; we will need a job; we will need this widget and that. We live to consume just to pass through a mundane moment... maybe the next moment will be better, or the next. From the outside looking in at society, we have the social growth and spiritual equivalency of Pac-Man. What a profound existence...

Freedom is not in what we have or can afford. It is not determined by an economy. It is not comprised of institutions, groups, or industries. We have decided that the existence of these things is imperative for a society to be free and for the American way to continue. Freedom is what we are, the life we can express. This freedom can result in amazing cultural advances, but these advances cannot be confused as freedom. Much of America has chosen the byproduct as the essence of freedom instead of realizing the origin of these things is inherent freedom. Our freedom can never be taken. It does not need defending. Utilizing our freedom is the only defense we need. For if we are truly utilizing our liberty, the liberty of limitless life within, there is no force than can rob it from us.

That mentality has brought about wars and famines, crime and suffering. There are hoarders trying to ensure they will always have enough. Living to survive something terrible, instead of being the change we wish to see, our light is turned over, given away and sometimes snuffed out. One cannot spread their light of truth and abundance while stockpiling in an underground basement. It's time to understand that abundance is for everyone, and only the illusion of lack trains us to witness otherwise.

Once we understand the power we truly have within us, there will be no sense of lack, for the true treasure has been found. Upon finding that treasure, there exists no situation in which you cannot endure just long enough for current, apparent destiny to change on a dime. In the blink of an eye, anything can happen. If you live and focus in hope, help will arrive.

The art of seeing only abundance can be honed by searching within. Our heart cries out for its own journey, that story ingrained within us before birth. Finding that story, which dances and twirls deep within the place our authentic self creates will sever the bonds that tie us to limiting thought, enslaving us to another person's perception or manifested, collective worldview.

Of course, all of our stories are intertwined. This does not mean, however, that we are at the behest of another's perception. It merely means that if we all follow the story written upon our heart, by our true selves, we begin to see a more fluid, cohesive manner in which our stories collide and mesh in harmony.

Immersing ourselves in another's creation can be so distracting, that our own story becomes fuzzy. Just because something exists, does not mean it must affect you, and just because something does not seemingly exist does not mean it remains impossible. The line between possible and impossible only exists within the constructs of mind. Learn to operate through heart and imagination, unlocking the most profound truths within, and the mind will become your tool, working in conjunction with your passion.

Practicing this will chip away at the false matrix provided by the rules of life, a paradigm set by groupthink or other external factors. Find what makes you the individual that you are, for therein lies your truth and your story. When the heart is aligned with its story, life becomes effortless and prosperous—whatever prosperous means to you. Your parents' or friends' idea of success or happiness may not coincide with your own, and that is okay. We all have our own stories. Books, magazines, and TV portray their own sense of what is acceptable success or truly possible, but they are merely another's creation and perception based on their hopes, fears, and life experiences. If you see something outside of you that rings true or makes your heart leap, it already exists within you and becomes a signal that you are witnessing a part of your story popping out from within to wave hello, beckoning you to keep traveling the path ahead.

Is desire a product of ego? Is the act of wanting overstepping the bounds of a set expectation of what this earthly life is? No.

Though we are programmed to concentrate on need, it is our wanting and desire emerging from the true heart that becomes the litmus test from which we can determine our next step. The heart needs nothing but the freedom to shine through the muck, and if our heart desires something, we have to trust it to not be egoic or narcissistic. When operating from our highest capacity, there is no need to fear a connected heart feeling selfish.

Here is a brief example: A man works tirelessly to feed his family, send his children to college, and take care of relatives that seem to always need some sort of assistance. His days are filled with the pressures of those in need around him. Slowly, his health starts to wane and his hope for his own dreams fades into what seems a childish memory. He begins to resent his career, but he cannot possibly switch paths due to those that "need" him, and the *assumed* risks that accompany the act of following one's true dream.

From the outside he seems noble, and though the intention truly is, what is nobility at your own detriment? Soon, being tired and weary transforms into exhaustion, despair, and possibly bitterness. This affects the body and soon could lead to him relying on others just as those relied on him, thinking all options are limited. Meanwhile, the guilt of not being able to take care of those existing in need also sets in. He is stuck in a vicious circle, created by the perception that others' stories supersede his own, becoming a martyr in vain.

I am not saying helping others is unnecessary. That would be heartless and ridiculous. I am illustrating an example where many get taken advantage of due to the ever expanding prism of lack. We feel that some are just unable to follow their own story, and so we carry their burden as well as our own. All parties suffer, consequently. Those that are dependent cannot break the cycle while the altruistic drown from the perpetual swim upstream.

"I can't change careers because...", "I need a break from work, but...", "I can't drop this or that toxic person from my life because..."—All of these "buts" and "becauses" mirror that programming, forcing us to look at need instead of our heart's desire. It is not egoic to say no, or choose to do for oneself. It is not selfish to wish to follow the yearning of one's heart. Your story, your life journey is for you, regardless of what others think or feel. They view life through their creation; you view through your own. Sometimes they line up blissfully as the two cross paths, and other times... we learn other lessons.

It is all so very simple in the end. Be where you wish to be—every day. Strip away the world of need in front of you. The mirage of lack has lulled us to believe it is a struggle and it's all a fight. Breathe easy and know it is all within—your health, your dreams, and all the love you need to fulfill an incredible journey. See the abundance, and feel the ease about you as you realize your freedom and empowerment.

The ears wish to hear a great story while our lips wait to spill theirs. There is want in that, and bliss. Our eyes desire to see the daily mural of the sky, and our heart dreams to be flying in it. There is desire in these things and a want that can lead us closer toward our story. Desire *can* be without ego. Need, however, is spawned by the illusory feeling of lack and is a great example of how the ego works. Lack is of the mind; abundance is the makeup of the heart.

As we awaken from our slumber and begin to realize instead of learn, anything is possible. We used to hear things like that when we were kids too... *Anything is possible.* What age was it that we dropped that idea for a seemingly better one?

There is so much sadness in the world today all because too few are finding their own story, and worrying about the story next door, or the fictional one on TV. Fear not though, because finding your story is as easy as starting to look. You are your own reality show, and I guarantee it will be far more entertaining, and far more real. I see more and more people doing just that every day, like you and me. Keep pushing past the fear, tearing through the facade of lack, which masks a glorious world standing not far behind it. You won't even have to strain your eyes to see it.

Remember why you're here, experiencing what you're experiencing. Trace it back, be the detective and find the clues of what got you this far and what you may have overlooked in the past. Go forward as if each second is a brand new creation of the universe. It's a clean slate every day, and there is not one person on this planet to which that does not apply. Forget what you think you have been or will be, and forget the same of others. Treat every one and every day as if they are brand new, and I guarantee you, yourself in turn will be renewed.

And forget that illusion of lack once and for all. All you need is within your imagination, sparked by that invincible heart. It then becomes obvious there was never anything to overcome in the first place.

What is Reality;
What is illusion?

Reality:
The totality of real things and events; something that is neither derivative nor dependent but exists necessarily.

Illusion:
The perception of something objectively existing in such a way as to cause misinterpretation of its actual nature.

We have heard teachers speak of illusion, holographic reality, and so on. What is real, what is not? I have heard some go as far as explaining that nothing we perceive is *real*, though my contention is that if *nothing* is real, than nothing could be observed or experienced at all. I could not write this, and you could not read this. We could not even witness an illusion.

If the universe was indeed "random" luck or coincidence, anything that could happen truly randomly lends theory that due to its unpredictable culmination it is without finite, unbendable law. On the contrary, we see that there is universal law that we can measure, show, and continue studying to further understand. This natural law or matrix can morph at any moment when need, intent, or cause exists for it to do such. Choices made by observable individualities of the whole, be it an individual cell or an entire being, determine the end result or at least the next step in the progression of the product or manifestation. These "choices" (and I say that these must be choices, otherwise all is on a predetermined path completely negating the possibility of a free-willed evolution, stemming from nothing at its onset) affect the others of the whole, minutely or grandly, therefore causing the other parts to make decisions based upon that environment. When enough unique decisions are made separately, new options arise exponentially as everything circles through existence, always expanding into new frontiers with yet another new set of possibilities or options. When similar decisions are made at a point of critical mass, whole paradigms can shift, cycles can change, and the creation-destruction model of theology and philosophy can be understood sociologically, bringing a literal understanding and application of assumed mythology.

The universe could not continuously expand without constantly introducing new concepts, matter, energies, or perceptions through which to observe these occurrences. It would become redundant and therefore would cease to be infinite.

Nothing in the universe is inert, ever. Even the atoms and molecules making up a wooden chair are in motion, though the chair is sitting in place. While I move my fingers across a keyboard, the chair underneath my butt contains a whole universe of its own, but it appears as a finite part of my individual universe.

The atoms that are arranged to form the material of the wooden chair is made of the same "stuff" of which entire universe is comprised, assuming that there was a Big Bang or similar original event that sparked everything. Therefore, my butt, attached to the rest of me, is no different in its most basic nature from that of the wood to build the chair. It all comes from the same "stuff", the "it", and its catalyst is imagination and intention.

If imagination is within us, separate from intellect, but a part of consciousness itself, it must be present in all aspects of creation, down to every particle or wave. Intellect is a measurable part of the fleshly aspect of our being, whereas consciousness would encompass will, emotion, and self identification and self actualization.

Consciousness, armed with imagination and intent as its powerful tools, is the active driver of universe expansion and change. For change is just that: expansion of what already exists. What we imagine is actually a true possibility that exists within reality, otherwise the very thought or image itself could not be conjured or observed.

The imagination and the images, thoughts, experiences that go with it, are a credible part of the universe. When you dream, visualize, meditate, etc. you do not extract yourself from the universe by doing so. Therefore, whatever is imagined, no matter how improbable, exists on some plane of existence past, present, or future either materially or ethereally.

If all was completely random, then imagination and the ability to observe any phenomena has evolved from absolute nothingness; a nothingness that was completely unaware of its own nothingness…

If this were true, there would have been no such catalyst to inspire a "Big Bang" or "Let there be light" event, let alone an evolving, ever expanding cosmos with multitudes of both individually and collectively recognized experiencing. Without this ignition, nothing could be nudged in any direction.

For example, we can build a "dream house" from nothing. It starts as we see or visualize it, based on what our preferences would be, possibly influenced by what others have built. This vision gets set into motion by intent or desire. There is then a swarming of creative expression and doing that happens, with educated engineering to blueprint and construct, and finally inhabitants that will live in this house. In a tangible way, this is the same process for the creation of anything, including the universe—through intention. If untrue, we would have, long ago, evolved past the pinnacle of consciousness at the original point of ignition, negating any need for progress or refinement as a choice or option in the nature of our being.

Why Create?

Unless we create, we would be at the complete whim of others' creations, existing at the behest of swirling, unfocused, chaotic energies caroming off of you and your seen and unseen possibilities. Some of your options become hidden, and the true solutions seem improbable. We then get swept up into someone else's world, the resulting experience is that of becoming a servant to their creation instead of being king or queen of our own; there would be constant confusion as to which reality belongs to whom—as is the case in much of today's society. We begin to identify with something outside of our selves by default—which would be an illusion of our true self.

Actively creating your own corner of creation and owning that as reality is the way to offset groupthink caused illusion. *Actively* is the key, however; you cannot avoid creating altogether. You are creating every single moment you exist whether by mental or physical action unto your environment. Inaction also creates your path forward. Inaction is a choice; *all* choice creates a new set of possible outcomes.

Creating allows you to see what is real and truly substantive to your journey, apart from the other journeys that are happening all around. Science cannot fully explain subjective experience, so it shies away. Computers cannot process subjective meaning, or create, as of yet, the same extensive atmosphere with the same amount of possibilities as the universe currently holds.

Subjective experience is the key to discovering the creation process through perception. This experience arbitrates all that will unfold before you, and if state of mind can determine such things as physical manifestations of the body, then consciousness obviously manipulates all matter and energy in which it has close contact. (However, physics has already noted the affects of non-local causality, so we can even say that close, physical or geographical contact is not necessary.)

The reality of illusion

Illusion is real; it can affect. The illusion is created in the same manner as reality, but subjectivity provides its relevance. Inevitably, you, I, and everyone else choose how we perceive the true nature of reality. It may not have to exist out of necessity, yet it does because it has been created.

Consider this adage: If a lie is repeated enough times, it will be accepted as truth. This is the basis of indoctrination, and in some way, large or small, we all have been subject to this. Indoctrination does not have to be malicious or intentional for it to still be effective and real. It all exists, true or not, but you can decide what creation or reality in which you participate.

We create things based on our determined set of ideals and laws. If the origin of where ideas are filtered transforms, existential paradigms evolve dramatically, and a new world is viewed. The previous still exists, but for now has no effect. The perceiver has chosen not to pay attention to the old paradigm, for it no longer serves the process of its realization or creation.

Simply because something exists, does not necessitate that it would have to affect you. You do not even have to see it, or actively experience it. This is selective perception, and by it, you choose your own creation, the reality in which you pursue your individual journey.

Nothing dies; nothing ceases to exist. The only thing required to bring it into reality is an observer to acknowledge its presence. Hundreds of years ago, someone buried a treasure. It is forgotten by its contemporaries, and hundreds of years later, someone finds it. It exists once again, but had the entire time, though no one had acknowledged its existence for centuries.

The illusion is only a false reality if it is not yours, does not suit you, or contradicts all that is within the understanding of your heart, and just because the illusion is exists, it does not mean it is "real" or viable to you. It becomes illusion only if it tricks us into thinking that it has limit or is the only key or option for your progress or invention. How you perceive determines whether something is illusion or truth, your truth. Your illusion could be someone else's truth, or vice-versa, depending on what is necessary for that subjective experience or awareness.

A mirage may not provide the bounty it appears to offer, yet the mirage still exists at least in ethereal form which will cause a response in a thirsty desert traveler; first excited, then disappointed, both causing a physical, *real* response biologically and emotionally. The *illusion* has a very tangible effect. This effect will provide a realization of some kind that benefits the soul, even if subtly.

Anything can be made real. *Real* does not mean it is either positive or negative, just as with illusion—it could be either. Although something may not exist today does not mean it never will. Furthermore, once anything is brought forth into reality, it will most certainly change. This is unavoidable. Nothing except the origin of creation is changeless. Things decay; ideas morph, fade, or expand.

All is real, regardless of physical manifestation. If a person knows something as an illusion, that thing does as good as not exist, for potency is removed due to, at its most basic premise, lack of interest toward said thing, event, or rule. Without focused intent, nothing can become tangible or credible. With the potency removed, one can enjoy the illusion for what it is and no longer be tormented by it.

Conversely, if someone is subjected to what they perceive as truth, despite its actual nature, they still can be affected by assumed results, i.e. the placebo effect during a trial for medicine. If the subject believes it is real, without any indication otherwise, the results can be impactful. The "fake" or illusion can produce real changes on the physical plane.

However, we can then realize that all on the physical plane is no more "real" than the illusory conceptions about these material things in question. When this is realized, the illusion can be transformed, making this plane more hospitable and without suffering.

So what?

So… if you do not take the reigns of your creative being, you will find yourself following a false, limiting paradigm of possibilities constructed around you by others' perceived "truths", tricking you into believing this is the way, or that is the way to accomplish a task, experience enlightenment, or tackle a problem.

Discern what your world is and is not. After identifying this, begin to create from your heart. This will uncover your story and bring it to life. In order to crumble all thoughts of limitation to create a new circumstance entirely, one must live with absolutely no frame of reference, or there will be fragments of the old paradigm that urges a certain limitation into your frame of awareness. Every moment lived is the moment of initial creation, the "big bang"; a completely new start and a do-over for whatever it is you wish to progress toward.

If we expect limitation, likening it to another previous life experience, we are accepting fixed boundaries based on mass-entwined creation. This collective creation serves it purpose in instances, but does not take into consideration the variety and dynamic of each possible personal journey.

The universe can be and is changed by one of the whole just as it is by the entirety of the whole. By this premise, Gandhi said, "Be the change you wish to see in the world." Your selective perception will determine your view of what is possible and impossible.

Obviously, the push-pull of competing and similar creations causes a pseudo-mutual mass creation, such as on a particular planet, region, culture, sub-culture, and other group dynamic of co-existence. However, above that group plane resides your plane where the manifestation of the heart happens and exists, preemptively manifesting among the metaphysical and physical, before conjoining in the co-experienced realm.

In coexisting environments, set paradigms may create a lapse of time between your ethereal manifestations and their physical occurrence in your world due to the rigidity and expected permanence in which *you* hold belief in the current state of mass experiencing and its ideals, structure, and concepts of natural law.

The steadfastness in which you believe something to be true or false will determine how powerfully you bring your imagination and visualization into reality. Extract yourself from the group paradigm and place yourself into the real you and your universe within. When the inner being merges with outward expression, you can move a mountain with a mere breathe.

The "Big Bang" is happening over and over, each nanosecond. You do not have to look back or recreate, fix or start over. Recreate your world today by diving within yourself. You are an ocean within your own being; swim its deepest parts and unlock the mysteries the masses profess are not there. You may reinvent yourself minute by minute if necessary, because in the end, you are not these things anyway, you are just an expression of the unfathomable amount of possibilities that exist.

To see reality is not to discard the illusion as though it has no meaning, but to acknowledge both the completeness of creation and your own truth, tucked within and in between.

Truth

Feeling truth is to witness it, not from the explaining lips of another, not even in the finite capturing of words in a book, for these too are subjective. One day the page is true until it has turned, as pages are meant to be, bringing a new page and a new layer of truth that can also be felt for a time, whether a minute or an eon. Ageless is truth, never dying once it no longer serves you, instead moseying on to emerge from the next heart, making its way outward to the visual or audible experience that affirms the knowing within them. Its bounty and revelation is what we all yearn for, in a world of swarming contradictions which confuse and cause unending lamentation about our existence and what should be done with it.

Truth is what is without limit or prejudice. Truth is objective, caring not if you believe in it, for regardless it will always be inseparable from you. One's truth can be another's misunderstanding, for its fullness is distributed to all, yet all see in their own capacity for openness.

It is found in both the illustrations of nature and the workings of man-created machine; though truth cannot be fabricated, it still exists among that which is, displaying truths explored and discovered by the builder, artist, or engineer, expressed anew.

Truth is for the process of application. Once it is found, it propagates abundance of life and universal expansion. Truth is not imperialistic, but nurtures the regions it sweeps through, finding those that welcome it while subtly, invisibly, and silently passing by those that refuse it.

Stark to those seeking it, soft and ever-present to those who have found it, truth settles in and becomes the infinite being-ness of creation, holding together reality and illusion like mortar for a brick home—two different sides of life, the tangible and abstract both having the substance of granite, are formed by each, but without either, all would be impossible.

If sought, we find that truth cannot be measured or compared outside of self; no numbers can be applied to its weight, or to height or depth. It has no color; it has no taste or smell except to the one who feels it and claims it as their own.

Behind every lie is the truth peeking out—one dog-eared page among five-hundred in a novel of fiction. In the hesitant flinch of falsehood, it is exposed in the stutter of a fabrication. Truth will ring clear and true, but only if you are looking, listening, and feeling with the sensitivities and prudence of your own heart.

Conflict Resolution

"Peace is not absence of conflict;
it is the ability to handle conflict by peaceful means."
--Ronald Reagan

There is always common ground. In the common shared by all exists the true self, that state of being that provides solution, maintains peace, and identifies with love and compassion, regardless of how the physical mannerisms or verbiage are expressed.

During process of conflict resolution, the goal of both or more parties shall be connecting to each other's authentic self. Behind the physical eyes lie the eye of spirit, past the physical ear is the one who hears without the ego which is wrought with fear and doubt.

Speaking and showing to this true state of being, embedded within the opposing party, provides an unfiltered, pure connection where ideals can be openly exchanged and personally felt. This is the seat of true resolution where progress is made even if the outcome is merely an understanding that disagreement of opinion need not escalate further than ending the conversation with a smile and a nod. Peace will then overshadow any conflict, proving there is nothing wrong with seeing things from a different perspective.

One does not need to compromise within oneself in order to achieve a balance between two or more opposing ideals. Both may be right, but rightness is based on viewpoint, and logistics can skew the appearance of solution. Know that in the end, we all want the same thing, though we express and experience it uniquely, causing the linear process to achieve this to seem foreign. This is only the mind trying to analyze the complex puzzle that is another human's mind and process.

The establishment of peace is not necessarily created without conflict. This has been a modern mistake by those with peacemaking intentions. The refusal to acknowledge and face conflict is escapism and fruitless. Sometimes there can be no calm without a storm, and sometimes we can appear to be calm when a storm brews within. To simply acquiesce in the name of peace is to allow the storm to continue raging beneath a calm façade. This is not peace. It is okay to dispute, fight, and debate. It is okay to sacrifice, to acknowledge fears, and to take a stand. This is where strength and courage are needed. It is okay to be right. It is also okay to be wrong. It is true wisdom that explains to us which one we are in a given moment.

Come to the table without expectation. Preconceived notions of those who sit opposite on an issue will only allow you to see in them what you wish or expect to see. Listen with the ears of your true self, and speak only words beaming from an unclouded heart. You will be heard, your hope will be seen, and so will theirs.

Make peace with yourself and all will be witness to this. The true negotiation has already happened within. Thus moments of debate should become time of communion, pushing aside the concept of a difference being a struggle. Each moment that is spent fighting against, preparing an argument for, or dissecting someone else's viewpoint leaves less time and energy to examine oneself. Realize your philosophies, do the work to unfold your story, and that tale of peace within will come bursting outward making all conversation smoother and better understood by all parties involved.

The things you just don't talk about...
Politics and Religion

"Freedom is lost gradually from an uninterested,
uninformed, and uninvolved people."
—Thomas Jefferson

At what point did we become uninterested, uninformed, and uninvolved? Was it the same moment we held too much faith in our government or a certain group of leaders? I have heard many people say, "Well, *they* know better than I about what is going on and how to deal with the situation..."

By what criteria does one make such an assumption, given the state of our nation? It stands to reason, if one finds themselves uncomfortable with the direction in which something is going, the last thing to do is throw up the hands and turn total care over to the faceless, unaccountable *they* to resolve our woes, especially if *they* are the very same that held the reigns, charting the course into the unpleasant state that has come to be.

Obviously a change is needed, and many start to accuse an entire system, a system founded upon practical, limited laws protecting, not providing freedom, for the cause of decline. Sure, we can wait until the end of terms, re-elect a new group of entitled "rulers", or we can address the real issue and the area in which we generally became uninterested, uninformed, and uninvolved—that area is our own self.

With twenty-four hour news, lightning speed internet, and the many social networking options at our fingertips, we are certainly able to plug in to what is going on. In fact, we are too engaged in things that are not genuine. Even the filtering of what information we receive as a public comes from a number of sources that have not been viewed as credible. If we are not receiving an accurate portrayal of the workings and events of the nation or world, how does a people discern fear-mongering from genuine scenarios, appropriately staying informed and armed with absolute truth, without attaching and concerning ourselves with every conspiracy possibility, tragic event, economic strife, and rumor of war that comes into our frame of consciousness?

This is where we start to unravel our current process of where we place our involvement. We have become, not uninvolved and uninformed generally, but detached from our very being. We have become wholly uninformed with looking within for these truths and answers to our largest problems. In doing so, we have let everything that passes our eyes and ears become another harbinger of an awful collapse, creating disenfranchisement and apathy flowing outward, creating an environment where it is easy to cow a nation of citizens into espousing anything—just to fix it. This outwardly visible apathy is a byproduct of the inward apathy. We would rather stick our nose in the business of everything else but our own hearts. Overwhelmed with fear, we retreat into meaningless exploit as escape.

The only remedy is to look within; find that greater wisdom, strength, and discernment, forgoing the tempting prospect of looking outward for the solutions and causes. Otherwise, we will continue to fall prey to buzzwords and snippets tugging at our emotional responses in order to maintain a status quo, as we quickly surf the news and media sites in the course of our hectic, daily lives.

Conspiracy: It exists. But let us move away from it—away from the worry and the frantic way it can fill our minds. Whenever two or more minds come together of similar interest and agenda, it can spiral either way—a great benefit to society by combining powerful, heart driven individuals to form any wondrous thing. Or they can decide to seek power and manipulate whatever they can for whatever end goal they may seek. However, there is danger in diving too deeply into such matters, for a cynical disposition befalls us. Soon after latching onto the concept that conspiracies are out there, one can get swept up, head spinning, seeing it everywhere whether it is or is not. This does nothing but continue the anger within, jaded nature of thought, and militant solution for a way out. The "at all costs" mindset is born. Meanwhile, the self is neglected, and the ego drives all of our creative aspirations for change, based in fear, anger, and hatred. (And remember: if there is that grand conspiracy, this is exactly what they would like to happen.)

This mindset also looks cynically at the grand divine conspiracy that exists for our betterment. There are those coming together by benevolent measures. Altruism can be mistaken for ill intended agenda. No good is accomplished by this cynical worldview but further destruction causing good people to do nothing.

The more we buy into the loss of freedom, fear of it, and struggle to keep it prevents one of solving the problem from within. No matter what is going on around you, you are the same, holding steady as others run about as though their hair is on fire. This is no way to find remedy or inner peace, which is the key to outer peace and a way to make the nightly news a little more palatable and worth the watching.

*"Our Constitution was made only for a moral and religious people. It is
wholly inadequate to the government of any other."*
—John Adams

Is it the Constitution that needs a change to conform to an evolving
society? It seems to be that it was written beautifully to protect the people
from rights determined by a government, rather than by Creator. Yet more
and more laws are instituted, and more and more of our culture decays.

*"Good people do not need laws to tell them how to act responsibly, while
bad people will find a way around laws."*
—Plato

No new law ever made man more free. The constitution was set up
to restrict government's ability to intervene on the freedom and creativity
of its people to pursue happiness. A government's sole duty is to provide
and protect and plot of earth for its people to pursue happiness in any way
they wish. By this standard, anything more than infrastructure and
pragmatic care takings of access to basic necessities, a military that is
never used with imperialistic intent, civil well being, and a very simple,
logical legislative practice, would be an excessive use of government.
There exists a growing, scary notion that the people are too dumb to find
their own happiness, or that the happiness they are choosing is
unacceptable to the whole. Who is it that decides what is good for the
whole? The result is an inorganic culture-molding body politic.

Can anyone outside of you tell you how you feel or what your
vision could be? Can anyone detail your unique way of expressing your
being on a piece of paper, written by lawyers, corporations, and
politicians?

Now some may feel that there is danger in such wide spread
freedom. The reason we have come to believe such an elitist mentality is

because we have lost conviction and right mindedness. Instead of searching for our true self, we sought selfishness and disregard for another. We cry out for our "rights" while refusing to acknowledge our responsibility. If you reject your responsibility, what good are your rights? Rights are only guaranteed by your responsibility, not a piece of paper, no matter how eloquently written and historical.

I understand "religious" from the above quote as personalized, not determining any prevailing ideology or philosophy, or any other single group paradigm that arises to power.

> *"As the government of the United States of America **is not, in any sense, founded on the Christian religion**—as It has in itself no character of enmity against the laws, religion, or tranquility, of Mussulme—and as the said States never entered into any war or act of hostility against any Mahometan nation, **it is declared by parties that no pretext arising from religious opinions shall ever produce an interruption of the harmony existing between the two countries.**"*
> —*Treaty of Tripoli, signed by John Adams*

You may be devout in any manner or by any religion, or not at all. One can follow a nourishing diet religiously, wake up at 5 a.m. to meditate and practice yoga, sit in nature, stroll a city sidewalk, lay back and stare at the stars or any of a billion other ways to add a frequent connection to the greater nature of oneself into the daily rhythm. We need a certain discipline about us; but that it constructed by the ways of the self, not by external uniformity. There is more than one way to eat a Reese's.

We have forgotten this. Partially because we have been told to think and pray a certain way, otherwise we are not accepted by that supposedly all loving God-figure in the clouds, watching, waiting for us to do something inappropriate. We become programmed to believe we are not worth it and are not enough, making us vulnerable to being consumed by our consumerism. A lifestyle is then sought to fill an inner void under the guise of being our ordained blessing from God for being a faithful nation.

Our nation has leaders who are involved in ideologies that take sides religiously and philosophically that lead us into foreign and domestic unrest. Currently, the majority of the United States espouses some form of Christianity. However, it is of utmost importance to recognize that our founders' intent was not the preservation of one religion or one lifestyle. They wished for freedom of religion. Religion is not defined as this one or that one. Many religions exist. All have their place and all have their shortcomings when exclusionary. Fundamentalism has been a great detriment to peace and progress, for it tends to rewrite the intentions of our founders and twist history to continually prove its exclusionary precepts. Our founders knew this, and this is why the First Amendment did not outline or mention Christianity by name.

First Amendment:

*Congress shall make no law respecting an **establishment of religion**, or **prohibiting the free exercise thereof**; or abridging the freedom of speech, or of the press; or the right of the people peaceably to assemble, and to petition the Government for a redress of grievances.*

It is very important to see that our founders wanted to ensure there would be no state religion. This is not understood by the Christian Right, for they do seem to desire a theocracy. By manipulating others free expression by labeling it an anti-Christian agenda, they wish to propagate the idea that their freedom of religion is under attack. Ironically, they are attacking others' beliefs. There are those, and a large number, who wish to hold up their scripture as law of the land. They hope to persuade the populous that the founders meant Christianity when they wrote "religion".

The founders' intent was exactly the opposite. They hoped that all would be free to exercise their religion as they saw fit. If you wish to have the bible taught in school, that defeats the very intent of the first amendment. The bible, in my opinion, is full of wonderful wisdom as well as great ignorance if taken too literally without reasonable scrutiny. If it is to be taught in school, it will step on the freedoms of others who choose a different religious philosophy, which includes those who choose no religious ideology.

If we are to be a genuine with honest debate and understanding of our differences, it must be said that it is not truthful to cry out about religious freedom when it is only Christian freedom that is your agenda. One is absolutely free to devoutly believe Christianity is their truth and abide by those principles. However, to direct foreign and domestic policy in order to assure it is the only prevailing ideology is an egregious assault on the First Amendment.

While fearing an Islamic jihad, Evangelicals wage a "civilized" philosophical war with missionaries, civil rights injustices, and fear mongering. When there exists an idea of a "chosen people" or an infallible scripture there will inherently be a bitter divide among people and cultures. This results in psychological oppression. It results in individuals unable to freely express their own religion or freely pursue their view of happiness.

There is not true liberty in a land that restricts the legality of expressed love between consenting individuals. To not allow gay marriage, for merely one example, is to restrict liberty of another philosophy or lifestyle—more accurately choice of expressing love. This is an assault on the very nature of the first amendment and is a cruel irony created by those that cry foul whenever their own freedoms are attacked.

When I refer to the John Adams quote above about the Constitution being for a moral and religious people, I do not attach it to one religion or philosophy. I believe it is important to find one's own path that is their guiding light in this maddening world. I see its purposefulness and beauty. Unfortunately, I also see its destructive ability when one group or religion professes its superiority. Religion is wonderful when chosen as an individual pursuit.

This is not to say that the anti-religion left fully understands the importance of the First Amendment and remainder of the Constitution either. It is time to respect each other in all manners, no matter the difference in philosophy. There has also arisen secular religion including health-conscious fanaticism that wishes for us all to be converted to a gluten-free dogma. Most espousing such exuberance are not even familiar with what gluten really is. Only those with Celiac Disease are truly affected by gluten, yet the fear driven, health industry has convinced many into needless worry. Climate change is obviously happening, but the cause is still under genuine debate, therefore forcing of the populous to adhere strictly to legislation before providing proof of cause is an infringement. Personally, I find climate change to be due to natural earth cycles, but not having irrefutable proof, there will be no demand from me to alter public policy.

There are many other forms of secular religious fervor that can be a detriment to freedom. We have made ardent religions surrounding many secular things in this country. Though there is no true *church* for many of these fear-driven ideologies, they are really no different than "End of Days" Evangelists running around clamoring about the world ending in fire.

It is also unfortunate to see atheists continually ridicule those that believe. There must be a mutual respect found among disagreeing parties. It takes just as much faith to believe there is absolutely no God that it does to believe there is one. Spirituality and science do not have to be mutually exclusive; in fact, many of the fathers and mothers of modern science were very involved in both, even dabbling in alchemy which provided a process still used today in some form.

In this country, we are free to believe whatever we wish. That is the beauty of it. If one wishes to believe only in science, that's awesome. If someone wishes to believe only in religion, that's awesome too. This is part of the spice of life. Let us not, however, let fear drive public policy and trends.

There is room for all kinds of diverse thought, none of which have to restrict another. This diversity of ideology can breed tremendous results for society. We can be open to new ways of looking at age old problems. We can come together and utilize our different worldviews to better understand our existence and societal processes. In the end, it comes down to respect of the individual. Let us remember, foremost, what it truly means to be an individual.

"The legitimate powers of government extend to such acts only as are injurious to others. It does me no injury for my neighbor to say there are twenty gods or no god. It neither picks my pocket nor breaks my leg."
—*Thomas Jefferson*

We spend more time desperately proving and defending our beliefs than actually living them. What difference does it make what your neighbor believes, chants, sings, or prays? Be blessed, sleeping soundly, knowing that they are spending time with that rather than peeking in your windows at night.

The thought that a certain belief expressed publicly or privately will undermine the spongy mind of a child or youth in general—well, that stems from a rigid process of constantly hiding one's head in the sand. For if that was a true possibility, no child would go off to partake in the usual raucous, sometimes risky behaviors youth experience for themselves. Yet it has been instilled in them to be careful and do this or that and not this or that, but they still do it despite good advice, proving that until one experiences on a broader scale than the thinking of the influential voices around them, they will not own such professed philosophies or advisements. Instead they live in a boxed, sheltered world of supposition. Where in that could true conviction and principle blossom?

Until they decide for themselves which belief system or way to experience suits them and their personal relationship with their creator and all of creation, it becomes a lazy, assumed, and unexplored ideology that serves them little, rather giving them clichéd and unattainable, externally provided, impossible measures of self-worth and prudence.

Yes, there are tragic, terrible things that our culture has witnessed throughout the country. These times have brought reflection upon our society and how its children are affected and the philosophies that are available and espoused. But above all, we seem to focus on, "Who is to blame?!"

Reactionary and impulsive, our minds led by fear, start to perpetuate all sorts of remedies targeting the supposed villains—regulation and laws passed, tighter security, and paranoid eyes watching everyone. These add more rungs to climb on the ladder, but do nothing to aid in the much needed healing. One cannot obliterate the past from existence, but stand to divinely learn from it.

We run from bird flu, swine flu, terrorism, climate change, unemployment, high-cholesterol, corruption, conspiracy, and tyranny. There appears to be a million and one things for which to be on constant high alert. We have assumed ourselves to be a frail species on a fragile planet. People from another planet would be stunned to observe us being afraid of everything in our own home. It seems silly to fear one's home, even if it is our home only for the time being, until our last breath on earth. What is there to fear? You have, at the very least, heard of somebody who's heard of somebody, who saw somebody on the news that has witnessed a miracle. Anything is possible in any situation—given that we remain open to new and virtually impossible things…

In the end, the answer is to create. If you are trapped, invent a way out, then look back and see you were never trapped at all. Looking within, you will see that which is truly you, and you will find, although scary at times, that you are inevitably an individual. Embracing that authentic "you" will lead you directly to the most creative times of your life.

If the individual is empowered and creating, experiencing their true worth, they come to understand peace even amidst turmoil and despair. There is healing in that. Whether gazing at a spider's web, drumming on a notepad at work, or sitting silently in a monastery, those moments are the same, sacred and free. You are connected and whole. Time does not exist; locality does not exist. In those moments, pain dissipates and that which is strong and undefeatable begins to take over and heal the wounds, moment by moment.

Taking these moments and the peace therein and applying them in this physical, manifested world ensures that your ideas and gifts shine through. That alone wards off negativity and illness. The physical body responds on a cellular level to every thought and emotion, thus finding peace within will even heal the body.

Expand that to a national or global scale; if we buy into the ill health of our people, we too begin to see nothing but sickness making our own bodies vulnerable, perpetuating the common diseases of our day. Conversely, if we refuse to dwell on the tragedy and illness swirling around us, pursuing only that of truth and peace, compassion and love, we soon see health and ingenuity abundant in our society, which in turn, will spawn new hope for recovery and long term peace.

This does not come about by boxing ourselves into a group ideal. No set of platforms by political party, no promises vowed through forced-smiling teeth, or national crisis—real or contrived, will bring us together. The answer lies within the individual genius of humankind. It will be unlocked by each heart following its unique story, fitting together in the larger puzzle without having to see the whole picture for their inner change to spread across the land.

History is filled with stories of great triumph and inspiration by those who were deemed crazy. The ones who left great marks on civilization were often accused of idiocy, lunacy, and heresy, only to ignore the naysayer and complete a life's work that led many others to find their own true calling.

We are not born in different places, from different parents, with different colors of skin, and philosophies in order to cast them off, becoming a mushy, homogenized group of gray sheep, walking in lockstep with the fad of the era, day, or season. We are born to be free spirited and creative. The very word creative is contingent upon ushering in something previously unseen. A rerun is not created. Regurgitation or mimicking is not birthing a new idea or invention. This causes stagnation and apathy. A lethargy sweeps over a culture that idly waits for someone else to create, while complaining there is nothing new under the sun and nothing good on television.

Greet each day as your own creation. Take the reins, making your way out of whatever situation that leaves you in discomfort. To create is to throw off the bonds of victimization; you are in control, as scary as that may seem from time to time.

Enslavement of a race has been abolished in this country, only to have its people, as a whole, voluntarily enslave themselves with heavy chains, forged from material stronger than iron—misconstrued thoughts of existence, and the doubt of empowerment from within. Shackled by perceived limitation and being ushered along nearly sleepwalking, we sporadically get swept in the rapids of public fervor for one stark, mass event or another, mistaking such for passion, patriotism, or heart.

If all lies within, as most of our religious texts allude, then what is it that tells us we are not enough, unable to create our way through anything with applied uniqueness of thought and inspiration? If one feels they are confined to the circumstances of which they find themselves, they have bought into an invisible prison and have ignorantly demeaned the heart and might of the divine spark. The keys to the locks of those chains are not hanging high above our head, far from the reach of our tiresome jumping, or buried in some archeological site yet to be found; instead they rest in the locks themselves, waiting only to be turned.

To turn that key is to direct one's attention inward, relishing in the individuality springing forth from the heart. In those differences of thought and perception awaits your harbinger. Therein lies hope for resolution, and once we dig past even that hope, going just a little further, the peace and joy we seek, that ultimate treasure, will reveal itself, nestled safely inside.

The way in which you are different from your neighbor is the bond that connects us together. If everyone thought, felt, and expressed in the same manner, by what miracle would new things be discovered on earth?

More and more, society elevates those that follow groupthink and single-mindedness. As long as we set up camp in the middle of a million marchers with a common goal, we feel safe and supported.

Be the one that lives the example of the inner workings and depth of the heart. Let that be enough, because if you have done this, you have done more than enough and your happiness will soon heal all of the emotional, mental, and even physical wounds and undesired manifestations. Connecting deeply with the true self will show you freedom that no new man-made law or provision can supply. All other ways have been attempted. It is time to love one's self unconditionally. In turn, you will have no choice but to love others, sensing the kindred nature of human experience. In this process, you have swum the depths of the ocean in your heart. There are dark waters. You will fight your battles there and overcome them, birthing a respect and compassion for anyone attempting the same.

You will see what you are made of through the story you have written and can appreciate the plight of others as they have a journey of their own. Everyone is living their own story, and all that is needed is a plot of earth, where people are free to uncover and enjoy their personal tales.

When we find our love in all things, we will find a strong, healthy society that fears no failure or crisis, corruption or apathy. We are many with many different views and backgrounds. For that to work, we must find compassion in every moment of our day—compassion for *ourselves* as well as others. Things are not that serious, seriously.

All that is necessary is to have that conversation within, with God, however one views God. If you do not believe in God, that's perfectly fine too. No one can deny the *I AM.* To deny it is to deny all experience. We all have consciousness and are aware of our existence. You cannot refuse to experience, and person can observe all that one reacts to or causes to be. I have seen an atheist smile blissfully and just "be", just as I have seen a guru or priest express the same. There is no one that avoids feeling closeness to God and creation, whether knowingly or not. Happy is happy. Joy is joy. Beliefs are nothing to get so worked up about. If you seek, you will find, and it will be in the perfect manner in which you feel wholly loved and accepted, complete and protected. You will feel the grand permission and encouragement to create the life written upon your heart.

It is yours and yours alone, regardless of what anyone thinks or does; you are you, connected with the all, and have every right to enjoy the beautiful gift of experiencing your own world, perceived through your unique eyes.

Some people know what they want; others try everything and find what they do not want. Every story is unique, every path is different, yet it is all sacred and leads to the same place—a place where nothing is sacred and nothing is all that serious.

"You cannot teach a man anything,
you can only help him find it within himself"
—Galileo Galilei

Hoping to convince another of the truth you believe does as much good as shouting at a burning house hoping it will stop the blaze. Sometimes, we need to burn completely to the ground, leaving nothing but ash, so that we may rebuild a better home. In that ash is a truth only that house knows for it is comprised of all that was before, now in its purest form with no structure to outline a supposed limitation, and no reliance on what was, leaving nothing but what could be. We then realize a greater truth and the new house will also burn and fall away. This is the pattern of learning wisdom throughout life.

Pushing onward through society as a salesman of hope, against opposition and ignorance, still leaves one a salesman; even if you may have a decent product to endorse. Anytime we try to persuade another, we immediately poke at the ego, causing it to be the causing drive of the conversation. Mankind must learn through experiencing, not merely hearing tale of it.

We rally against this or that, perpetuating the fear that the thing we fight vehemently against will usher us to our demise. Truthfully, it is only the fear that hurts us. It speaks to us through our most intricate thoughts, and we hold it up as logic. We cannot do this because of that, and that is not possible because of what so-and-so has proven. All that so-and-so had proven was that it was not *their* method.

Showing someone the way to look within will show a truth that needs no convincing; one that is owned by the truth seeker, thus more genuinely applied and cherished.

Anytime we see or hear something that resonates, we are experiencing a truth from within. It is already a part of our being, familiar. All truth and wisdom lies within and only searching for that authentic self will unlock it. Then it will be made apparent in everything to which you turn your eyes. Soon, you cannot do anything without experiencing the truth, and all that is false will irritate at first, but soon fade away as though it does not exist. This is because you choose only to be among that of the truth and wisdom. Even the foolishness of those around you becomes understood, and therefore the urge no longer exists to correct or instruct.

"If everyone is thinking alike, then no one is thinking."
—Benjamin Franklin

We are not alike. We do not think alike, yet we seem to have fallen into a belief that it is time to convince each other that there is a right and wrong way to think or be, and to fix things, we need to all get on board and think on the same side. If that was the case, there would be no use for think tanks or focus groups. There would be one genre of music, very few books written, movies produced, and cultures thriving throughout the world.

It is not about groupthink. The expression of the many moving parts and ideas within the group allows for those differences to shine light on societal problems. Limited government provisions and brief, logical legislative language that is without cryptic loopholes and exclusionary remarks can free the ingenuity of a people. All modalities can be accommodated without infringing upon natural law. It takes many different angles of thought and expression to develop and sustain an enlightened, versatile culture.

We worry about who is thinking and believing what or whom, when it is a miracle of life that we even think!

"If all printers were determined not to print anything till they were sure it would offend nobody, there would be very little printed."
—Benjamin Franklin

When was it, exactly, that we lost our edge? We have come from pioneer days, rugged individualism, overcoming a national depression, and surviving earth shaking wars to build a feat of mankind, among a free people, to a modern day where people take so personally, a mere insult from another person, whether it be by word or term, illustration or gesture.

Be it the media, politicians, entertainers or the guy next door; it seems we are all on the record every moment of every day. Who, I wonder, is this perfect being? Is there some sort of tally at the end of it all where a person is only allowed "x" amount of gaffs, slurs, or general mistakes?

One wonders why we no longer have legitimate statesmen with a decent shot at becoming elected. No one with any sense wants to be held accountable for a harsh or silly word they used when they were eighteen. Thus, we only get those without sense.

If these words hurt so deeply, it is time to look within and pluck out anything negative or hurtful plaguing you; then release it to its origin. Pay no mind to what anyone thinks of you. Let go of the programming of societal paradigms that poorly allude to self worth and achievement. Cling to your individuality and your path to the divine. Being rooted in this will make even the harshest racial slur bounce harmlessly from your armor.

Know that falling down is okay. We all have indiscretions and have let silly things fly from our mouths due to anger, drunkenness, and overall daily pressures mounting. Refuse to buy into the punditry and status quo of holding ourselves to this standard of outwardly proclaiming we are doing okay. Inside, we are all fallible on this earth. This, however, does not keep us from having pure heart and spirit.

You are better than the world makes you feel; look inward for the world you wish to see, and live it as though it has arrived. Fear not the slip ups in which you may find yourself; the time to worry is if you have made none lately… You will know by this, you have fallen into a routine.

It is just not that serious of an ordeal, this life. It is blessed and a miracle, yes, but with enlightenment and remembrance of who we are lying so closely as within our hearts, it stands to reason that only *we* can let ourselves off the hook for the things we have done. It is the least we can do for ourselves—that part of us that just begs to poke through, showing you the way of your story and the peace and love it carries with it. Ben Franklin also said, "Hide not your talents; they for use were made; what's a sundial in the shade?"

You know what you bring to the table, and if you do not, remember those moments where you were caught dazing off, and whomever saw this asked, "What are you thinking about?" and for the life of you could not explain, with any words or gesture, for you were not entirely sure yourself…

This is where it all reveals itself, slow and subtly, silently and nearly missed, and then all at once in a bang for a moment. Then in a blink, it is a wonder if it had happened at all. Go to that place of silence and complete stillness; investigate the real you.

The authentic you carries no concern over who hates you or other opinions of dissent. It is all understood for what it is, and bears no weight for you to carry. If your eyes are forward, they will have their opinions and absolute freedom of speech, and we will have ours.

Freedom requires dealing with some nonsense at times. We do not have to fight hand to hand for our opinions or perceptions. The tough battle is letting a word be a word and an offensive comment fall aside. It is time to be mature and keep our eyes forward, showing our light by the lives we lead with unmistakable joy in our eyes and smiles. When a man stands on a cliff, yelling at a man on the other side, he does this only hoping for a response; even when the man is alone and yelling, he yells to hear the response of his echo.

We can approach hatred and negativity as though the bringer of it is merely trying to hear their own echo. With the proverbial "water off a duck's back" mentality, one day it will cease. With no response but an echo, why would a man go hoarse?

No word or idea or pairing, grouping, flock or gaggle of them could possibly do any more damage than we allow them power. Sometimes the truth is not easy to print, for it seems to rattle and disturb our fragile sentiments.

Every day, someone is complaining about what someone has done, said, or thought about doing or saying, and the day we finally move on from this, we immediately relieve a huge burden of what holds us down.

I think we have given political correctness a fair shot, and it's accurate to say it is not working. Tensions get higher among this and that group, and for what—to remove more ugly words from our vocabulary to save money printing dictionaries? It is time to hear our own echo for a bit; finding what it is that makes us so raw when someone "hurts" us with language or display. Instead of using time to better our self and rise above such pre-teen, dramatic reactions to anything to which we disapprove or fear, we have fought vehemently against foolish voices carrying vitriol that makes not a dent in our skin or moves a hair from our head.

If we speak freely and allow others to do the same, the shock factor will dull, and life could move forward without fear of even the slightest experience we endure or decision we come to, in and for that moment. Let the hateful voices finally go hoarse.

"Democracy never lasts long. It soon wastes, exhausts and murders itself. There was never a democracy that did not commit suicide."
—John Adams

A beautiful society had been created, as many had before it. Freedom sprawled and then receded; so goes every era of all mankind. Marvels of science and industry turned to ignorance of truth; instead of a harmonious partnership came the days of self destruction shrouded in the empty promise of apocryphal progressiveness.

Apathy, fueled by earthly comfort, lulled the masses; soon they gave excuses for the misgivings of those elected to serve, who decided to serve themselves and not the people. This is the way the individual dies, a family withers, and a nation squanders the benevolence of God.

We had forgotten the work that comes with a blessing of grace, and now shout to the heavens as though God had forgotten us. The amnesia took the diligence and responsibility, replacing it with hardened hearts that look upon irrational, unsustainable principles, propped by seemingly good intention. This merely masks the guilt. Sleepy heads need to sleep, and the tossing and turning ends no matter the conscience, when one becomes exhausted enough.

And so a great land became lesser, due to heartlessness in the workings of its people. We are heartless toward even ourselves, for we chose a slow suicide, far more gruesome than going up in a nuclear flash. When one hates the self that hatred turns inevitably to their neighbor, for it cannot remain hidden for long. Festering inside, it must manifest outwardly and nastily.

To return to a day of great progress in American society, we must return, not to the state of mind of our predecessors—for time brings about the evolution of things—but to their state of heart and passion to evolve. Their hearts longed for freedom and were willing to commit to the daunting tasks that lay ahead. They searched within for strength and hope. Far tougher than facing the oppression of King George was facing their fear within; diving into the depths of their souls to come together, despite many different beliefs and personal sacrifices. They were bonded by the heart calling for the pursuit of true happiness which can only be found individually. Discovered in the silences of the day, finding the inner workings of one's own story in solitude and bringing that forth into the deliberations, a declaration and constitution formed to ensure all would be assured freedom under such framework.

Today, we debate over historical record and who meant what when writing this or that. Heated debate and compromises ultimately happened in order that all people, walking many different paths, would find their own path to fulfillment. We should celebrate and study the process of such framework, for in lieu of the many differing opinions, they were able to capture on paper the spirit of a soul's journey and what proper place government holds along that road in one's life.

A man has nothing if not for his distinct dreams and unique quest. No signature marked upon that constitution looked the same, neither did their ideals. It was broad and generalized, not so it could be obscured and easily changed, but so that rights remained inherent and not allocated by other men with other agendas.

It was simply constructed, albeit through a painstaking process. Provided in the Bill of Rights alone were fundamental guarantees to ensure no man or group or nation could squash humanity's progress toward a "more perfect union". They knew nothing constructed by man would be impervious to malfeasance, but developed during those unsettling times was a system to allow people to create their own model civilization. The only fear was, as had happened with every democratic system since the beginning of time, the people would soon become apathetic as life became easier and more prosperous, and domineering men would take advantage of a people that settled for government safety nets and entitlements over the diligence of looking within and performing the self-work necessary to sustain such a grandiose idea of a nation—a nation structured without tyranny deciding the whole of their days.

They created an environment in which a man or woman could fly or fall, solely based upon whatever they wanted and happened for their journey. A place where our stories could be played out, unhindered by rulers, was forged dawning generations of hope and unsurpassed progress.

Alas, we stand at its waning hour, the great experiment. What is going to bring about an actual reformation, and let this experiment live on into an even greater era, defying history? The answer rests within you and me, by going within, connecting to who we authentically are, in our divine nature, and healing ourselves. When it awakens, all will be healed and it will flourish once again.

At this turning point in civilization, we can awaken to a Renaissance if we nurture the precept of "all things are possible", or we can revisit the dark ages through time-proven ills such as doubt and "sheepdom" and blind groupthink.

There is a grocery list of devastating scenarios and reasons for our worry including environmental, geo-political, and economic. How can we conquer them all? We could not, in the current style of diplomacy and conflict resolution.

We must only change what we can... ourselves. That, I can promise, is difficult enough on its own. There is no need to look outward, searching for other houses to tidy; look within, metaphorically vacuum, evaluate the decor, sort your DVD's, and finally get to those windows. Flush the rain gutters, sew a garden, on and on until all is refreshed. Rejuvenate you, mind, body, and spirit.

A world full of beings doing this will conquer all of the perceived obstacles separating us from peace and prosperity. And all of this is done without lifting a sword or legislating utopia.

Today, genuinely searching within has become more terrifying than an asteroid hitting the planet. You're told you are unworthy. You're told you cannot do this or that. You're too sick or unfit, too feeble to survive your natural habitat, yet powerful enough to be able to kill the planet.

You're too poor or too rich, to skinny or fat. You don't believe in the proper God; you don't believe in the right politics. You don't drive the right car; you don't have the right clothes. You don't love the right person or hate the right group. Nothing you do can be worthy of anything. Why would you want to examine something as terrible as your own being?

This is the paradigm that most experience today—a life of lack and happenstance beyond any control or inspirational value, for we are the accused vermin of the earth...

Know you are worthy. Live your life by your heart's purest expression. Disregard any rhetoric teaching you otherwise. That paradigm has led to a depressed, diseased society; a society that hates itself. This hate will cause it to die—cultural suicide.

The solution to suffering is to know all things are possible and that you are worthy of them. Do not believe you are incomplete in any way. Wherever you stand, whatever you may understand, whatever you feel is perfect for this precise moment in your life. Tomorrow can be changed. Know this moment for what it is, what can be learned, what can be experienced, what can be enjoyed, and what can be painful. This moment is only a culmination of all the moments preceding.

This moment is the only time you can alter the coming steps on your path. If you worry this moment, a worried hand sews the seeds of tomorrow's bloom. If you are hopefully present in this moment, your inspiration will come and you will manifest with joyous confidence and excitement!

Live as though you've forgotten the newspaper. News, be it good or bad is old news as soon as you've read it. If you can change your next moment in this very moment, who could not? Hold nothing to expectation, greet every moment as though it were the first moment of your life. This is your creation point and a clean slate every second. Everything changes; *how* it changes is up to you.

The "Sheepdom" of Man
is Without...

"Forget Conventionalisms; forget what the world thinks of you stepping out of your place; think your best thoughts, speak your best words, work your best works, looking to your own conscience for approval."
—*Susan B. Anthony*

Millions wandering about, pushed by howling winds down hollow streets, are frightened by their own shadows cast out over cracked pavement and dry landscape. They witness only impending doom, lack of opportunity, and thieves gathering around waiting to pounce on the very last bit of self they still own.

This is the sheep mentality we have come to embrace—a populous more concerned with the exterior goings-on than the interior nuances and messages of creation, embedded within each soul. We look to others to gauge our expression, cautiously measuring appropriate displays of our feelings. Without another's blessing, we find no validation for the thoughts swirling within our minds. Hoping to substantiate our feelings, we prove in desperation that we fit in among the mainstream, praying to not draw too much attention to our quirkiness or exposing the silent struggle of self-acceptance.

We watch the television and either buy into the depravity and sadness or cry accusation of conspiracy. We look at our neighbor with squinting eyes, peering through their smile, assuming it comes from some place of judgment when that judgment has been pouring forth from only our own minds. Scared to death of our imperfection, we project our inner demons onto an unassuming scapegoat—that other soul that is merely trying to navigate their own choppy waters en route to their own enlightenment.

Busied by trends and gossip, we seek any validation that can show we are okay and better than the ones around us that are visibly crumbling. We immerse ourselves in our gadgets, creating higher walls deflecting communication and expression, further concreting the illusion of society that people are inherently evil, unintelligent, and easily cowed into panicked survivalism. By viewing the masses as lemmings, we see the sheep mentality that is present within ourselves, should we let it take over by shifting into complacency.

We stare far too deeply into acts of terrorism and war, watching the shadows that live within us playing out on the grand stage, delivered by people in suits and haircuts who are just as scared as we, perpetuating the false reality of lack and doom. Only seeing what we fear, they only report what they fear and we believe. It is simple supply and demand on a metaphysical level, rearing its head in the papers, the internet, and the nightly news.

We want desperately for a villain to absorb our mass blame. We want to identify the ideology, culture or expression that creates all of the turmoil, so that we can continue avoiding that which devours us from the inside. By viewing it within society, we numb ourselves to it all happening within us where it actually gains power.

The war, the oppression, the hatred and fear originates from our own minds. We then extrapolate these battles onto the mainstream, collectively throwing these visions and obstacles into a big pot and watching it manifest. Region by region, neighborhood by neighborhood, person by person, we all begin holding our breath, waiting for some external hero to defeat our internal demons.

It is a difficult thing to admit we are causing our own angst. There needs to be a villain, so we choose one, lambasting anyone who was merely acting out of their own fears and self-imposed limitations.

Why does a man strap a bomb to his back and blow up buildings and innocent people? Is he evil? Is he mentally ill? The ideology that has spread is that by performing such a violent act, that act may not in turn be done to you. The fear of a group of people taking what you hold dear can manifest into these atrocities. We all hold fear, and some let it consume them with such ferocity that it spurs such unbelievable actions. Yet we have deemed them unworthy of compassion, instead wanting a villain to judge for our insecurities rather than identifying that we too, have the same fear of usurpation, attack, or obliteration.

So we shuffle along, handing over our fears to an outside source that will be willing to defend them, for they too fear our common fears, and make decisions accordingly.

While a group of elected officials seemingly let things slip away into injustice and tyranny, we must realize that they too live with their own shadows. We wish to demonize those that use poor judgment. Someone MUST be held accountable! For what, making a decision through ego? This is an act to which we all succumb. Somehow it is inconceivable that someone in office could make a mistake or fall to corruption of power! Why? Have we held them to some higher standard than we hold ourselves? Are they superhuman, elite beings that are infallible?

Or are they simply people, like you and I, merely trying the best they can, sticking to their own belief, at times rooted in truth, other times rooted in false precept. Human beings are susceptible to corruption. We are not less than them. We are not more than them. We fall and they fall, all based upon following what we falsely believe to be truth.

Even the most radical ideology, making little sense to anyone outside of the fold, has believers that truly believe they are right, therefore they will act accordingly based upon that philosophy. This, although misconceived, is not out of evil or a desire to injure, but is manifest out of a sense of needing to be free.

There exists evil in the world, but it rarely comes from the source to which our eyes have been led. There are those that claim to have awakened to what is going on, alas they have just awakened into yet another dream. As society labels this or that as being THE evil, true evil outsmarts us by keeping the collective mind several moves behind the shell game. There is no money or political power to be gained in getting to the true root of the manifestation of evil. It can only be vanquished by each individual ridding it from their lives; therefore, there is no Hollywood scenario to grip our attention. Coming to our own personal awakenings, defeating our own fears, and living authentically may be difficult and revolutionary work, but it is far less appealing to voters and consumers on a mass scale. There is nothing for the corrupt elite to gain through this type of battle.

These corrupt elite are asleep as well. They have based their thought processes on untruth, just as we do in our own lives albeit on a smaller scale or at least a private one. They maintain power and continue to drive fear by having the people point fingers at their own neighbors. We continue to chase nothing but ghosts, hoping one day there will be liberty and happiness if we destroy the public demon.

These ghosts are personified in the opposing viewpoint or political enemy. We assume the other side is evil and wishes to destroy our nation. We have been convinced to believe that if we are right, they are wrong and there is no gray area. Everything is black or white, good or evil, right or left, up or down. There leaves no room for compromise. Compromise would be giving in to evil, leaving our "convictions" behind. Ironically, our convictions are meant to be our own, and by leaving it at that, we can live by our convictions without making others hold the same. Other than radical, fundamentalist sects of religions, no belief system calls for *forcing* others to hold the same convictions. The true nature and intention of religious beliefs is for individual benefit and living, *not* for the manipulation of collective behavior.

A liberal, wishing to have social programs for all who are in need does not actively wish to drain the pockets of hardworking people, merely their focus is placed on those who are hurting and they place their priority and principle of governing on such beliefs. Whereas the conservative's priority is in ensuring the hardworking should not have to pay for others' sustenance except by their own charity, not by governmental ordinance. To the liberal this will appear stingy and selfish, while the liberal's philosophy will seem to the conservative as though achievement is being bastardized. The argument ensues and we come to a place where heated rhetoric and demonization drives us further from the remembrance of what a constitution is for. It is a format unto which all parties and beliefs are accommodated when we throw aside the fear that the other is out to destroy our way of life.

Instead of both coming together to find common ground and apply a checks-and-balances of thought and policy, gridlock ensues for neither side will see the good intention and wisdom of the other.

There is a balance of push-pull in the universe. The pushers feel there needs to be more pushers and the pullers feel the need for more pullers. The truth is that both are needed to hold it all together. There are truths in all ways of thinking and even among opposing ideologies, truth will be found on both sides. No one person or group has a monopoly on the truth. Conversely, no one has a monopoly on the lie. We all hold accountability for that, through buying into the limitation presented by our minds working overtime to solve problems that were only solvable through the ways of the heart.

Even an apparently evil, oppressive king truly felt he was in the right, regardless of how perverse the train of though may have been. Every human being bases their actions by what they perceive to be genuine;

otherwise they would not have the perseverance, passion, and accumulate the resources necessary to enact such expression of their unique core belief.

This is not to say that bad, destructive ideas should not be debated and fought. Rather it is the manner of which we debate that is in question. Are we listening to our opponent, or merely waiting to jump in, explaining to death our own talking points? Do we open our hearts along with our ears, understanding that even if the other party's thinking is misguided, the angle from which they arrive and sincerity therein may hold some sort of insight as to how to smooth out our own incubating concepts?

Once we realize that our opponent is not our mortal enemy but may indeed hold a different piece of the puzzle, there will be productive compromise. Even if unfit for the particular issue at hand, we can start to embrace different solutions and compromises where necessary. Otherwise, we shall continue yelling at each other, claiming we are the only ones who get it, and painting dissenting opinion as that of buffoonery or an intentional undermining of society. Compromise is not bad. Poor compromise is bad.

We have separated ourselves on opposite sides of the street, yet on both sides the sheep are walking in line, following someone or something that even slightly resembles our principles. It is time to be those principles instead of mimicking those who speak the loudest about them. By living our personal, unique ideals, we become them. When we become them, there will be no need for the nudging of society into what we or a certain group wishes it to be.

Live who you are and what you believe. This does not require you to make others believe or identify with the same. In fact, doing so will remove you from the path of living that which you already are and were always supposed to be.

Refuse to follow others into the state of doubt and fear, compromising your story to appease the fears barking inside your mind—

those watchdogs of common experience alerting you that this is uncharted territory. Chart your own course, following only the feeling that dwells in the heart. This feeling carves out a path in which only you can determine its benefit and worthiness to your end goal. This path may make little sense to your logical, thinking mind, for it only knows what keeps you safe. The things it has not experienced bring signs of warning, keeping you from experimenting, forever in a state of fearing failure. The mind has trained you that failure is finite and brings unbearable consequence, when in actuality it has only brought you to a place where you can then decide to modify your path and evolve. Use your brain, but be not trapped in the mind.

Our greatest discontent is brought to life by comparing our story with another's. Yours is yours, and in your own heart rests your only haven of understanding. It is the only place that one needs to look for answers and validation.

Perform the difficult task of looking within, and end the passing of the buck. No one is going to show you your way, no matter how enticing it may seem. It is okay to be happy, even if your happiness appears alien to the person beside you. It is okay to not have every answer readily available; answers come as they are needed to be applied.

Struggle not for words to express a feeling of personal truth—no amount of explaining will bring someone on a different wavelength to yours, no matter the vernacular or eloquence. When they are ready to receive it, it will be felt within their heart, just as revealed to you.

It is okay to be viewed as different. Is it not difficult to merely follow the status quo, day in and day out, decision by decision? It is a daunting task to bring to concrete form that which has no form. Instead of living as the round peg in a world of square holes trying to cram into a safe place either by force or by changing one's shape, know that you need no holder to be held. You are intact.

Forcing yourself into what you *think* you should be instead of just being that which you are causes discomfort and brings unnecessary burden to your path. You and all of your notions are not fixed and unyielding. Creation has changed and continually changes, and if you believe yourself to be a part of creation, it is okay to deviate from that which no longer serves you. Holding on rigidly takes effort; an effort that consumes energy better used for the creation of your own story.

We have paid too much attention to the many stories playing out around us, becoming entranced, captivated by others way of being and denying ourselves the right to acknowledge our own answers.

Opinions and advice, although offered through well-meaning lips, are only examples based upon the findings of one individual through their chosen adventure. Some of which may apply to your situation while most are just other options, not representing the totality of ways any path should or could be traversed.

A mountain to climb is ahead. Those that have climbed it previously offer maps and strategies in which they were attuned along with tales of dangers to avoid and shortcuts to the summit. You, however, may wish to fly straight to the top, and even though none before you have professed or accomplished this, it does not dampen the possibility of your vision. Trust your own chosen path. Advice comes from another *mind*, delivered by a soul that may sincerely care, but is not connected with what your heart sees.

Buying into the mind's fears and created, insurmountable obstacles constructs a wall of self-doubt. If this self doubt triumphs, you may avoid the mountain and its adventure altogether, leaving you forever wondering what may have been in store for your spirit and experience.

Either be nudged along the chute of society with the other sheep in a direction that stifles your story in an unending circle of lack and need to be compared and measured, or take the reins of your creation, and be that which defies common ideal and produces uncommon result.

"Life's but a walking shadow,
A poor player, that
Struts and frets his hour
Upon the stage, and then is heard
No more; it is a tale told by an idiot,
Full of sound and fury, signifying nothing."
                    —William Shakespeare

How sad, the thought of this, a hollow life of fret and acting, biding time until the final curtain closing. It is a mindset that plagues many as they see things falling apart as storms circle. Gritting our teeth and doing the best to mask unsettledness and confusion, we don the mask we find, acting out desperately trying to show that everything is fine despite the empty feeling left by a disorientation to the significance of a life.

Though a beautifully expressed grouping of words by Shakespeare explaining the contrived nature of a particular life, forced and unfulfilled, this is not the manner in which the true self wishes to be expressed. If these words make you respond, "Exactly!" then take time to explore the vast mystery and meaning of life and all that must come together for you to take even one solitary breath, eyes opened, and with the ability to observe a happening.

Here lies hope among a crowd of actors. Here lies emptiness, not of insignificant nothingness, but an emptiness free of burden, fear, and expectation—free from the stuff we collect that is not of who we truly represent in this skin. We then transform into a vessel that can be filled with love, adventure, and mystery.

Victims and Victims in Waiting

No one is the unluckiest person in the world. God does not pick winners and losers; it is you who choose whether you triumph and fail, as well as the purpose either could lend.

Being open to the lesson puts you in control of happenstance, allowing yourself to see the story of growth and opportunity, even amidst tragedy. Humankind has thrust serious conclusions upon fleeting moments. Spending time calculating ramification and consequence, we turn a world of trial and error into one of judgment and punishment. We must now live for experience and apply experience toward realization. Trial and error are wonderful guides.

To claim victim-hood is to deny any involvement while validating that you have been defined by said experience. This is as effective in breaking traumatic cycles as being hit by a car, confusingly staying in the middle of the road, yelling aloud about the time you were run over.

Step back from the road and watch the traffic. Watch yourself getting hit. You will discern the points of safe passage for your next crossing. You will observe your own ability to control that which seemed previously uncontrollable. Slow the traffic and read the license plates; find the steady flow of all that is. In that flow are things that could potentially run us over, drag us along, or simply illustrate the ebbs and flows of life. What you experience depends on where you place yourself. Are we standing in traffic looking for a way out or standing along the road, looking for the proper path and timing to cross?

Victim-hood breeds hopelessness and perpetuates the outlook of randomness in an unkind universe. It is not random. If one thinks this way, it is merely because the time was not taken to align with the messages and connect the dots before proceeding. The signs are all around and stark if one chooses to look. This is being present.

A healed scar can tell a great story and be a proud reminder, but hardship and great tragedy can be experienced without carrying an open wound as a badge of identification. Let the result of overcoming the tragic moment become a badge of honor and an example of inner strength; not by dwelling on the moment of turmoil, but by letting the beauty of growth and proof that humanity can march forward. Allow yourself to blossom for those around to see you move from status of victim to victor.

You are the happening, not that which is happening to you. Shifting this perspective will allow you to take control of the situations that come along your way. Be it a national tragedy or personal struggle, buying into a cyclone of negativity or doom and gloom, lets you dwell on how it happened. This causes fear of it happening again, pouring excess energy into preventing something that already had passed, keeping us in alert mode. In alert mode, we avoid the healing process and never address the original trauma.

Live free, burdened not of worry and apprehension, but empowered by hope and fortitude. Let others worry frantically about the next horrible thing bound to come our way… they merely have not let go of the last thing, viewing it for what it was worth. Let them foolishly come up with ill-conceived remedies that restrict freedom and cause continued paranoia, while never addressing the healing needed to turn society's "self" around.

If we are to hand over our power saying, "It's their fault; they did this to us!" We have already lost that battle; giving our personal sovereignty over, negating all of the teachings of the wise that came before showing us how to find enlightenment and refuge from the ills of the world. It's not about escaping; it is about realizing there is nothing to escape! Once this is recognized truly within the self, you will see you are always protected and no one can protect you better than you.

Buying into the constrictions of a fearful society of victims and victims in waiting will propagate paranoia and stress which will only spawn new physical, psychological, and emotional illness. This never gives us the chance to throw off the uniform of the victim.

There exists a darkness that wishes for you to never know how empowered individuals are. Your imagination, your light within, the love and compassion you can emit is all that it takes to do away with having to continually learn the hardest, most painful lessons of earthly life. Quit letting the mind be the most effective terrorist our individual worlds ever experience.

We all know those people in our lives where everyday is the worst day of their life. Our nation has become that person if we are to buy into the news media or our politicians' rhetoric. And they are correct, as long as we continue to let that be truth, hold it in our hearts and live accordingly, scared and beaten, acting as if human beings are too frail to make it on our own and too naïve to read our own signs to move forward. This is the greatest lie ever told, that we are not enough and that we are not safe. You are safe. Refuse to be a victim or victim in waiting.

Finding *YOUR* Way

What is it that sustains us? We pray, meditate, look inward, and stay active through exercise and sports. We eat properly, perform our responsibilities, and try to be a light for others. Even with these tools to sustain our peace and fulfillment, sometimes it is difficult to feel the presence of our authentic self, the divinity within, and that all in all that is.

Storms swirl and uncertainty pops up from moment to moment. Busy lives and busy heads keep us doubting, fearing and losing touch with that feeling of wholeness. Feeling that we've somehow lost what we had found during some spiritual journey or endeavor as we venture onward into the day to day, the elusive bliss we seek is only elusive because we forget the feeling inside. Instead we depend on visual or tangible beacons in the world around to let us know it is still there.

What good is the majestic sunset if not for the feeling it gives? The view is splendid, but would it be so if there were no accompanied glowing within to remind us its origin? The thrill of a rollercoaster, dropping our stomach as the wind rushes past our ears shows us the thrill, but is it the external or the internal where the thrill originates? Who or what is feeling this?

The internal is where it begins and ends. We well up with joy through certain activity, but it is not the activity per se that provides, only mirrors what is within. Therefore, if the sunset fills you with bliss, that bliss is already within. If the rollercoaster wraps you in adventure and thrill, this may only be so if adventure and thrill is also within.

The only question to ask oneself when choosing what activity to evoke your nature of being is, *what is it that allows me to feel what already lies inside, patiently waiting for acknowledgement, even as we are impatiently searching for it?* That impatience and frustration only comes to us when we look outside firstly, before finding that truth within and then choosing to express what we have come to find by doing.

It is overwhelming to imagine sitting as a monk 24 hours a day in utter bliss and enlightenment. A lot of spiritual guidance portrays this state of consciousness of one of zero doing, no interaction with the physical, fleeing from it as if it were a burden, an involuntary luck of the draw. But when we push past attachment to the physical activity and merely observe it as an expression of the bliss already found within, we find that it is not necessary to just sit in endless meditation to sustain that feeling, but we venture into the physical world with an observatory attitude, watching that which dwells in us manifest right before our physical eyes, ears, nose, taste buds and skin. This is what life here is. See this incarnation as a lesson-rich, once in a lifetime journey, full of more possible twists and turns than anything on television. It is your story, written upon the heart.

Too often we try to escape this physical life through our spiritual practice, assuming it is the final source of enlightenment and all tangible is that of distraction from that which is divine. Conversely, it is that which we experience physically which is the proof of life and enlightenment. You can not avoid experiencing. Can you choose to not observe—even for one moment? With eyes closed and floating in a vacuum, you are still experiencing, at the very least observing one thought or a million. Simply choosing *what* to observe is the answer. Even this process seems to choose itself effortlessly. We seemingly will ourselves to and fro, place to place, person to person, experience to experience. This is life unfolding. This is why we are here.

Your story lies within the things you choose to see or feel. Of course, we need to spend time in solitude to recharge and reconnect, but staying there for too long does no good for your path without sustaining that peace throughout your physical, daily journeys. What is the difference in your consciousness while in meditation as opposed to at work? Are you not still observing all that is going on? Do not the same principles of clearing the mind and living in that distinct, unique moment still apply whether sitting in the lotus position next to a koi pond or slumped in front of the computer entering data? Are we suddenly different beings depending upon which of these locations are experienced? The mind, processing different stimuli tells you things have changed, but your heart reminds you that it is all the same.

The same person visualizing being in a forest, birds chirping, sunlight trickling through breeze shifting leaves, bringing serenity is the same person standing on the busiest city street, horns blaring, tires screeching, people briskly brushing by our shoulders, bumping and pushing along. You are the same in either place. You are in control of what you experience by how you perceive said experience.

If something uncomfortable comes to your frame of consciousness during meditation, for example, do you flee it? Can one go to another state other than solitude and silence to find greater peace? The same holds true to an annoying or frustrating happening in the walk-around part of your day. Something winds us up, and we feel the only thing that can help is to run to a place where we can meditate or decompress so that it does not get the better of us... Well, what is the point of that really, and why are we not sustaining our bliss and oneness?

What is it that prevents us from that bliss during normal 9-5 existence? The answer is the mind. Use the same tools during that hectic moment as you would during meditation. There is no need to escape or seclude. The actual escape is merely the knowledge of this. Be the calm in the midst of the storm. We can sit in silence and be plagued by our thoughts, or we can be among a crowd and be plagued by our own and others' thoughts. Both are quelled by the same stillness within; a stillness that never leaves you for one second after you have come face to face with it during your spiritual times. It is carried with you; in fact, you are actually carried by it. It only takes a shift in recognition, constantly remembering you are that stillness and bliss regardless of what is hurling itself toward you, swarming around you, or scampering away from you.

You just are. Period. There is no caveat; no but, no and, or if to this. You cannot be injured or hindered. You cannot be suffocated or set back. The true you is eternally at peace, and only when we forget that truth momentarily, the other stuff in which we falsely identify ourselves will lead us away from realizing this unending peace, but we can come right back immediately.

There is no struggle; there is no need to fight. We are just experiencing this for a moment for the lesson therein. Acknowledge the lesson and return immediately to that *you* which is utter bliss, strong and impervious to that which surrounds you. You are what is deep within, not that which is without.

Just be. It is very simple, but we make it complex. Someone comes with trauma, tragedies, physical pain, tumultuous home environment or what have you, and saying to them, "Just be," can evoke such frustration and lead one to cast it all off as mumbo-jumbo that becomes a meaningless, prop of semantics. We get caught up in the *"ism's"*—the groups in which we lump ourselves, but those *ism's* are merely stepping stones, a meeting place and archetype that only illustrate a portion of how to evaluate and experience existence and our place in it. These are beautiful expressions of all that is, but are not complete blueprints. We have to find our own way... It is time to find the *"I am"*s". Instead of the *is's* of, "Jane **is** hurting", "John **is** angry", "**Is** happy", "**Is** sad", find the **I am**. This is you. Any other tagline past the "I am" is a modification added upon the true self which needs no modification to be found or identified. One is not mandated to fast or chant to find that I AM. This does not mean it is not a worthwhile venture, but if we start to believe we MUST do this or that in particular to find it, than we are saying we are not enough without any physical or mental alteration to the ineffable I AM.

We learn to tie our shoes through formula or catchy little rhyming song that reminds our child mind to perform the steps necessary to tie that bow and keep our shoes on our feet. Soon, though, we no longer sing that song, make the bunny-ears, etc to complete the tie. It just happens without conscious effort. The bow is tied, and now we move on through the day.

In the same respect, enlightenment can be found. Sometimes we need a mantra or a candle, a quiet place and 20 minutes to meditate, or a song, a scripture or whatever it may be to train our mind to settle into that place. These are all wonderful things and there are a million more ways to choose from, too many to list. However, once we have ingrained them within, it becomes like tying that shoe. It just happens. One's routine may stop being of service at times, causing disbelief in the magic of said tool or "ism". This is not the case; the magic still resides within that modality, but you now do not. If it has served its usefulness and now is something that you "have" to do to find enlightenment, now instead be free to find *your* way. The magic is inside of you. Take all that you have recited and learned throughout your entire life's searching and know that it all resides within and had long before you started this journey. Tie your shoes without thought... or stare into the loop bunny ears in bliss. Either way, now or in any moment, one can "just be."

Optimal Health and its Origin

Health—One of, if not the main issue concerning our society is swimming in our heads from sun up to sun down, and we find our self chasing the proverbial wild goose trying to discern which path to take in order to unlock our healthiest self. There is no study needed, no experiment necessary to prove, that a healthier you will improve all areas of your life, mentally, creatively, emotionally, and socially. We see that every day.

Where does your health come from? Modern thought mixes genetic and external factors for the bases of most procedural medicine, diagnoses, and therapy. Therefore, this creates the philosophy of dodging the things you cannot possibly control to attain optimal health. Play your cards as dealt.

Many people, including medical professionals, are continually awakening to the obvious defect in that philosophy. Science clearly shows the effects of stress and poor diet. This is obviously a major area that *can* be controlled. So why are many people, when shown the benefits of happiness and good nutrition, choosing to be unhealthy? Yes… I said choosing.

Where does the line end, though? At what point do our *choice* and our predetermined *"luck"* fork in the journey? Or does it?

The philosophy to which many are turning new eyes is a philosophy of many ancient cultures, and much of these are still practiced today all over the world, and now starting to boom in America. Ironically, the Native Americans practiced much of this, so it is hardly a new concept to our soil. These old paths are being explored again, and we have all been hearing about the necessity of mind, body, and soul balance. If these are aligned, one can assume good health. (…and "REsume" good health as well).

I see the change ahead, and have been blessed to see it working everywhere, daily. There has been a shift in how we view our health and well being. It is a change deviating from the current thinking that has proven to be ineffective and costly. The economics do not make sense; neither do the results and efficacy of some modern paths. There are a lot of new possibilities ahead, with limitless reason for optimism. We just need to find that balance.

But what are we balancing? Well, mind, body, and soul. Are the mind, body, and soul one? Should they be treated as one? Is there a ring leader?

The body is your physical, flesh and bone stuff that maintains all the processes you need to experience life on earth. Consider it the grand machine, but do not dishonor it by thinking it only mechanical. It is very much organic and alive. Honestly the body can be the pawn in this game of life, at the mercy of the mind and the soul. At the same time, it is our temple and the very vessel that makes this incredible journey possible. Both seemingly insignificant yet indeed a keystone of life; it is the first thing most see of our being. It is what plagues or boosts us. What is it a representation of? Why is it the way that it is, and to what end or purpose? It is this: Our poor physical health is product manifestation of the struggle derived of disconnect between our mind and our spirit.

The mind, oh the mind… What a cathedral of human evolution!! We hold it up, saying, "Look!! Look at what this blob of grey matter can do!!! Oh, how we have come so far as a species," when in fact, the brain is a computer. The brain is *not* the mind. I would put it in the same category as the body, except for a tricky little thing. The brain can be programmed by both external and internal stimuli… A computer that can program itself! This is where the mind comes in. That is, if you let it continue on, set to a certain frequency. It goes about its business, controlling all of the involuntary goings-on within all of the bodies systems. Usually, we are only aware of it when it acts up, bringing us to analyzing and thinking, or distracting us from a task. Sometimes thoughts of worry or pressure arise. These are all constructed by the mind, using the brain to sense and process all around it. If left unchecked, it will do its best to keep the physical body safe, but it will program the brain based on a paradigm of fear. In reality, the mind looks out only for itself and the body can be left to fend for itself.

The brain that processes conscious negative thought also programs the involuntary actions of the physical body, right down to the cellular level. Science has found that peptides are released according to different emotional states, triggering immediate responses within EVERY cell in your body. If staying in a state of perpetual depression, your cells will be programmed thoroughly and react accordingly.

Take that a step farther… The same mind that thinks a negative thought, also controls the subconscious, and if habitual, decides the workings of the involuntary processes of the body through the wiring of the brain. One of these processes most immediately affected is the immune system.

If you continue on a negative or depressed, fearful or angry pathway of thinking, each cell grows and performs according to these signals, hormones, and peptides released by the brain. If that source is corrupted through negative emotion or thought, the molecules released for normal function of systems gets constantly mixed with those negatively thought provoked, survival triggered compounds, therefore ensuring the outcome at the cellular level to be less than optimal—at best.

Imagine a river being fed both by a beautiful, clean spring from one side, and on the other side, runoff from a toxic waste facility. Is not the whole river and whatever it feeds into poisoned? "Oh, but by the time it gets to me, it will be diluted… Only just a little bit of poison…"

Well, that little bit of poison continually feeds those recycling cells, from birth to death, day by day, month by month, on and on. This is what we are building our bodies with, using the very basic building blocks of life. They deserve the best start they can get.

So, it's virtually two on one against the spirit. The spirit, despite its current dwelling, is a free flowing embodiment of light. It is connected to pure consciousness. Despite popular belief, you are not your thoughts, or your body. In fact, 98% of the cells in your body completely regenerate in less than one year. (Collagen and cartilage take a bit longer.) Therefore, the only thing left standing that is truly you, year by year, is your consciousness—intact and never affected by any physical change. It stands to reason that the only unchanging, eternal part of you is the best place to start the reprogramming process, en route to controlling the mind and manifesting the physical health you deserve. Yes—deserve.

By connecting regularly to our spirit, which is more intimately connected with pure consciousness, we can bypass the negative reactionary mind, infusing our health with proactive choices that benefit our physical being.

Remember earlier I mentioned "choosing" poor health? At this point in society, with all the education available, it's only responsible that we come to the recognition that many people are choosing poor health. Working in the fitness and health field for the last several years, I have heard every excuse why someone cannot make a workout appointment or follow a better diet. From "I don't have the time with work and this and this…" to "My kids and husband will never eat that, and I'm not cooking two meals…" There are a million reasons in between.

Think about that for a minute…

I know we live in a busy, uncertain world. We have placed so many demands on ourselves, that there are no more minutes left even for our own basic well-being. At the end of the day, as our aches and pains grow and we complain about the unsung power of an M&M's addiction, and our pants don't fit, can't sleep, sad all day and night, anxious, nervous, itchy, flaky, watery eyes, nasal congestion, spare tire, and on and on and on… At some point, we need to look in the mirror and stop making excuses. Why do I not have ten extra minutes to eat a healthy breakfast? Of course, you do have time. It's about wanting to utilize the time.

The likelihood of ten more minutes of sleep doing anything to drastically alter your day's productivity and/or happiness is silly. Here, we are choosing to skip breakfast for something inconsequential. It sounds silly, and it's easy to shake my personal trainer finger at you and say, "Now, now, you certainly know better," but what does that really accomplish? Nothing.

We are deliberately CHOOSING something rather insignificant over very basic needs, proven by the most basic of sciences of how our body works.

The fact is, and a slightly jarring one at first to most people is this: For whatever reason, and one that can be pinpointed only personally through inward focus, you somehow feel you are not worthy of caring for your body properly. Somewhere along your journey, your mind became programmed into thinking the trivial mattered and the important does not. How and why did this programming happen?

It all comes down to self realization. Once you realize who you truly are, you can then take the reins, ignoring the programming of the mind's conscious negative thought, while reprogramming all of the involuntary processes that need balancing with positive thought and expression. You will see how much you truly deserve the highest possible health! Once knowing this, it will be harder to make the excuses…

This is the future: Connecting to spirit → control of conscious mind, producing healthier sub-conscious → healthier sub-conscious mind sets in rhythm all of the body's processes, naturally, and organically, allowing us to make better lifestyle choices. We need to stop chasing that sick wild goose and tripping over our bandages. Go to the source of it all. Heal our spirit by owning it, recognizing it as our true being-ness, and being grateful for it. That is where our true health resides.

We had been going about it like this: Physical body shows symptom → Diagnose and treat symptom; if symptom persists or worsens, spreads to other areas, etc. → we *might* trace it to the mind → once we get to the mind, we end there. Good luck.

As we start to observe our thoughts and set new patterns of positive thinking, so will be the same process of each cell in your body. Imagine practicing this for an entire year… Every cell of your body will have been placed by a bricklayer who cared so deeply for their home, that nothing could invade or disrupt its bliss. That is optimal health.

Economy

"You only lose what you cling to."
—Guatama Buddha

A man loses his job. This is the axis point of change. These axis points crop up daily; a charge to redirect energy and intention, expanding a new set of grand possibilities and reevaluate our priorities.

Change brings with it a discomfort as we try to process and proceed, moving through uncharted territory filled with uncertainty, and though we have been unsure many times before, every time it happens again our mind reacts as though this is the first time we have lived through change.

An economy rises and recedes, like the tide or a breath we inhale and exhale, sometimes settling into a state of imagined normalcy. We witness life in all aspects evolving continually of large and small scale, yet we discriminate as to what should affect us and what should necessitate worry.

The economy of a nation will reflect its ability to harness free flowing ideas into fruitful operation. As necessity breeds invention, the ability for people to apply their creative assets with as little restriction is the key. This fertile environment comes from the individual as they realize they are not bound by concrete trends of an amalgamous, ever mutating culture.

You are only subject to a passing trend if you buy into it, letting the brain dictate the interpretations of rules and finite possibilities of any idea. If we wait for the economic environment to change, by government action or intervention, we resign our most precious assets, our ideas, to either wilt or over ripen and spend excess energy on the concerns these situations superficially present.

The government can do nothing to spark growth through trying to level a playing field, attempting to control ever fluctuating, normal trends, and imposing the belief that this is the way it must be.

"Government's view of the economy could be summed up in a few short phrases: If it moves, tax it, if it keeps moving, regulate it. And if it stops moving, subsidize it."
—Ronald Reagan

This is how government, looking at a populous as an entire, faceless group of bipeds, knows to aid any arising situation; it completely disregards the prospect and potential for one idea to change the course of everything.

There will be greed and there will be naivety to feed it. Conversely, there will be altruism and proper self-interest, and will be wisdom to seek it. Rules which are constructed by government inhibiting the ability for one to choose to be guided by greed also inhibits one who chooses to be guided by altruism. Thus we end up staying in static scenarios, unable to move far enough in any direction to truly try and fail, stumbling upon new avenues of inspiration and the products resulting of such.

Run quickly from the professed situational status of anything as a collective, including an economy. You may lose your job, your business, or your nest egg. These things too are never permanent, guarded as sacred and unbending. For neither is the discomfort of unexpected change; this too is passing and but a fleeting moment of introspection and new attunement. Embrace the opportunity for a different way forward. This is life's way of jolting us into new frontiers, providing a greater capacity to progress and fulfill.

If we cling to what we think should always be, what boredom would ensue by not making room for a brand new collection of possibilities and experiences?

Foreign Policy is a
Foreigner's Policy

"Everyone thinks of changing the world,
but no one thinks of changing himself."
—Leo Tolstoy

Why do we create policy for something "foreign" to us?

Policy: *A plan or course of action, as of a government, political party, or business, **intended to influence and determine decisions**, actions, and other matters.*

Other than determining how we wish to express and present ourselves in view of other nations, we should have no hand in dictating any policy directly influencing the matters and elements of a society outside of our physical border. To shine our example requires no reaching action. Otherwise, we are infringing upon another people's journey in realizing their own purpose and individual freedom in how they wish to experience and express their spirit either as an individual or a collective culture.

Even "spreading democracy" has shown to encompass a sort of infringement, embodying, at the very least, a taste of imperialism. Imposing how a nation should structure itself causes an unrest, for it is not wholly homegrown, ignited by their own people, who are the ones that will have to live in the political environment formed outside of their direct influence and own discovering, implementation, and nurturing.

When we try to live up to, be contained in, or formed to a preset expectation of structure derived from an external source, our mind tells us we have fallen short, no matter the progress attained or fruit cultivated. A form concocted by anything other than that which is within can never fully become brimming with a total sum of its possibilities.

There is no form that can safely contain, without inhibition or injury, that which has no form, the spirit. The spirit must form its own dwelling and its own policies while developing its own capacity to detach from both. No nation, regardless of how grand or enlightened, can determine such for another.

The "shining city on a hill" is not to send out its glaring laser-beam of light that blinds people through their windows, but is to be a silent, beautiful example of only what is possible.

Education

"I have never let my schooling interfere with my education."
—Mark Twain

What have you learned that is most valuable to you, and where did it come from? Was it a mathematical equation or how to spell chrysanthemum? How about the date when pilgrims landed on Plymouth Rock?

Most of the details are forgotten if not used semi-regularly. We plug linked tidbits of information into our pliable yet overstuffed brains like bytes of data uploaded onto a mainframe.

Memorizing, calculating, analyzing, cramming for tests that show, for that block of time, we have retained certain information in order to move on to the next level of standardized intellectualism.

To fully grasp a concept is not to memorize the details and logistics. People learn differently and learn best in an environment in which they can feel the concepts unfolding around them. To memorize and spit out information as though we are mobile data storage devices does little good for a being that was born to create new ideas and manifestations of abstract inner knowledge. Educational regurgitation, as a teacher of mine once called it, does nothing but arm a generation of parrots that can recite a plethora of facts and figures but strain the mind in doing so, leaving little room for comprehensive applications of limitless possibility. We are not on a fixed foundation of knowledge to build upon that is without flaw or bias. Nothing *must* be this way or that as the measure of a person's education, by today's standard, seems to indicate.

Educational regurgitation gears the brain to take in, commit to memory, and spit out for the use of scoring a certain number of correct responses solely for the purpose of expressing items that are already known and researchable.

"Never commit to memory what can easily be looked up in books."
—Albert Einstein

We base our educational worth on a standardized test which eliminates the prospect that intelligence is expressed and gathered in a multitude of aspects. Each mind is unique; each story has a non-uniform way of unfolding and merging with the whole. No two students are identical.

We scramble trying to fix an educational system that, by uniform measurement, appears to be lagging behind other countries of the world. Let us disregard the fact that all we are doing is comparing our capacities for memorization, not application, and take it at face value for this particular "dilemma" our nation fears.

"More funding!!" is usually the proposed remedy for all social ills, especially education. This is the solution espoused by most Americans; the result of lazy politicians who think by clamoring for more funding into a certain system it then shows them as crusaders on behalf of the youth of our country. Is more money the answer?

For the figures below, keep in mind that we are comparing standardized tests and their scores, nation by nation. Here are statistics from 2011 illustrating how much taxpayer money is spent per student for education:

South Korea: $3,759 (2nd in math scores worldwide)
Finland: $5,653 (1st in math; 1st in science)
Japan: $3,756 (4th in math; 3rd in science)

Canada: $5,749 (3rd in math; 2nd in science)
United States: $7, 743 (10th in math; 9th in science)

*Sources:
www.cia.gov/library/publications/the-world-factbook/index.html
www.geographic.org/country_ranks/educational_score_performance_country_ranks_2009_oecd.ht
ml

As it shows, we are currently spending much more each year, per capita, with no indication that it is the key to higher scores. We are spending a significant percentage more than countries excelling above us, as per test scores, yet our main argument and remedy is to throw more money at the problem…

If other countries are spending less and achieving higher scores, to what do we base our logic? I assume we have forgotten to memorize that logic is important.

How many other issues do we assume more funding is required for a fix? Somehow, somewhere along our road "more funding" became our only viable solution to all that ails us.

Why? It is easier to write a check than actually apply the ingenuity and creativity to enact open-minded, multi-faceted approaches. In order to do so, that would require less time and effort spent on re-election bids. There are too many fixed minds, built on rhetoric and pandering, unyielding to new concepts and broader-scale thinking. I am not proposing to not spend money on education. We must look closely at how we are spending it and scrutinize the very philosophies of educational process in order to be satisfied with our purchases.

Our neglectful orientation to cookie-cutter solution has created cookie-cutter thinkers, pressured to keep up the preconceived notions of their abilities and how to enact them. This causes redundant thinking and application of stale techniques and archaic rehashing, none of which can propel a society into a new frontier.

Alas, we become trapped in a worn out cycle of stagnation and frustration. The result is disenchantment from a learning process by the pupil, and the increasing boredom of a generation.

Compared to other nations, we have never had a problem funding anything truly worthwhile (setting aside our debt issue for a moment). It is the implementing, for which we have been absent, in fact, negligent and lazy. It is time to learn a new way to teach, and teach our youth *how* to learn instead of what to learn.

Teach one another to ask, "Why?" and watch a new set of "hows" bloom, pushing us past even the greatest difficulties we face.

The Kingdom of God
Is Within...

It begins and ends here; the concept of concepts and the truth of truth. The rest seems more like window dressing. Whichever spiritual path, philosophy or identified religion you may belong most likely speaks of this understanding: The Kingdom of God, Nirvana, Paradise, Bliss, Moksha, The Source—your only road to it resides within.

Somehow we still find a way to externalize, either sending our prayers and hopes skyward only, hoping they reach the clouds and beyond, unimpeded by swirling winds and dark clouds that seem to block the outgoing prayer or incoming blessing.

Has the white bearded man, light-years away been slow in checking his email? Is your voice too feeble and falling well short of His throne?

We know that all is within, but why have we pushed it aside? Whether a family hardship, health concern, personal uncertainty, or any other painful experience, we tend to watch and wait for help to arrive, long before the understanding that it was here all along.

When owning the infallible truth of the kingdom being within, all that *is* originating in your heart and expanding inward and out, we will change the way we view the world, our place in it, how we pray, deal with our minds, discern our inner messages, and approach the pursuit of joining our true selves, and awakening to that joy.

Take time to meditate, focusing only on that truth and the powerful message it carries. For God is genuinely within, sitting on a throne in the middle of your own heart, surrounded by all of the magic of creation, expressed through you, by you, allowing you to observe and experience while fulfilling your own personal story, learning your own personal lessons. What can we not overcome?

If the source resided externally, we must hope our prayers are heard or even cared for, praying yet another prayer, wrought with doubt, hoping to assist the original prayer toward its destination. However, if the Kingdom of God is within, there is no waiting, there is not one unheard or misinterpreted utterance from your heart to God—there is a direct line. This is where true empowerment dwells. This is how we know that all is truly possible.

No one needs to save the day; all is already saved while knowing the love, the strength, compassion, and magic resides entwined with our being. We are never without. We are never too weak.

Realizing this, fear begins to wash away; now we know all is heard and taken care of; we merely have to show up and believe, smiling and being as your heart instructs. All is at peace within. What could possibly be left to cause serious worry or doubt? When focused on the indwelling divine, there is no concept of death or mortal judgment. God is as likely to condemn you as you are likely to cut off your own finger for picking your nose.

All is forgiven. That which is not forgiven by mankind is forgiven by God. It is because we do not forgive ourselves that keeps us hurting, angry, stressed, sick and frustrated. We fret over national tragedies shown over and over and over. We forget our timeless nature when we get too wrapped up in awful things shown for exploitation and programming, political or otherwise. We demonize humanity, and being human, by proxy demonize ourselves.

We mourn the loss of things that naturally pass away, and not release the grief fully. We hold on to things that are not eternal. It's time to turn to the immortal part of our being, take a deep breath and cut ourselves a little slack.

It is not that dire. Nothing is ever too far gone. It is not all that serious in the end. Sometimes we fly, sometimes we fall—all of us. And we have the unconquerable, timeless divinity within to guide and protect if we merely listen. God would have no cause to let even one speck of Him fade into obliteration, wilting and dying as the physical body inevitably must.

Shift the focus within to that which is unending and all powerful. Instead of continuing the search outward, begin uncovering that which tucks God away from our vision—our *stuff*, our yuck. All of the false programming, rehashed negative memories, and frames of reference that fog up the window to our own soul get wiped away, allowing one to see their genuine nature of being in its most pristine state, pure and divine.

The only demons that stand in your way are your own; take comfort in this because if they are yours, you can know them as illusionary products of the mind and more easily face them and let them fall away, leaving a clearer path inward toward your authentic self. You know these things and more importantly, feel them. You have them closer to you than you have your teacher, pastor, guru, priest, rabbi, cleric, shaman, swami, or family. They are inside.

You hold the keys to the kingdom of God. You determine the combination of the lock; this is the truth, for you have created the lock. The truth was hidden in the hearts of humankind where no man could corrupt it, mistranslate it, or throw it away.

Revolution

The scary images the very word conjures—citizens rising up, civil unrest, military coups, violence in our own streets. These are completely avoidable, while still ushering in a much needed, drastic change to our way of governance.

Groups have tried violence and protest alike, yet with little difference to our political climate. Debates over facts and opinion get tossed about, full of egoism and panicked rhetoric from politicians and special interest groups vying for the thoughts and votes of the electorate, in order to prove their validity.

The results are endless, redundant laws that provide less freedom and continued worry over which way to navigate a legislative matrix to find which route to happiness we are permitted to explore.

While "they" keep you focused on the ills of a system, no focus is left for gratitude and no time remains for applying ingenuity. They have been able to convince Americans that its government is the entity that provides, while only taking. No new law ever made mankind freer, and words on paper do not save us from those who already disregard the law, common conscience, or even common sense.

We have been cowed into believing our rights come from allocation by government, indirectly from the decided need of the public collective. This philosophy hinders the creativity and effectiveness of true hearted citizens, yet changes not the heart of the law breaker.

Those who disregard natural law will do so, no matter the amendment or reinterpretation of a Constitution. Not one law has changed a heart, only stirring up new dissidents and with it, a new battle to fight.

It is time to spend sessions of Congress removing redundant and restrictive laws. It is time for our public servants to view themselves as such, providing a service to the people.

The only service required of them is to protect the first ten amendments and provide a plot of land that is safe from threat to its people, providing an infrastructure that is suitable for the uninhibited pursuit of undefined happiness.

This happiness is undefined so as not to exclude any path. Happiness should not be appropriated or mapped by an elite few, popular theology, or altered by the illegitimate fears of a provoked collective. One person's happiness, though appearing alien and unfit to another, is their own, and is sole property of the individual. You own nothing of another's right to pursue what they wish, and they own nothing of yours. Likewise, government does not own or create your rights, therefore they in no way lay claim to the ability to allocate, change, or revoke. However, without responsibility, you can certainly give up your own rights.

In issues of economy, we have seen industry boom and regress, not based on a new law, regulation, or executive order, but merely by the thought of what a new administration might do. This fear causes people and businesses to react without any tangible stimulus resulting… just supposed, assumed and magnified fear that does more to stop progress than will the stroke of a pen pushed by a lawmaker or lobbyist, desperately seeking the approval from a skittish people who are cynical and tired.

Government produces nothing, yet has fooled its people into believing it is the only source of resolution. Therefore, a revolution against a governing body does nothing but oust a formal, external savior for a new one—at which point no real progress has been made.

The revolution is to be within, where the true power resides. The battlefield is in your mind. Use your heart as your shield, letting it go forth before you lighting your path. Fight the voice within that speaks of limitation; revolt against the programming that foretells doom, gloom and dire need.

Turn off the TV, and line the birdcage with the newspaper. Spend that time in blissful ignorance to the flailing incompetence and external battles of the confused and hardened.

Know that your salvation comes from no other place but the internal eternal. Quiet the chattering mind, push through the doubt and find all of the tools for breaking unwanted bonds are at your disposal. Fight in your own solitude and then come together to commune in peace with the individual resolution that has been found within.

A group of angry, scared citizens creates nothing but confusion, drowning true solution from being heard; but a group of settled, self-aware individuals can come together and fortify their light and emit peace and abundance into a world thirsting for change.

That change grows organically from the most fertile soil of the soul. It is not "change we can believe in" for change occurs whether we believe in it or not. We are required only to seek it for ourselves for it to manifest as a quiet, compassionate, loving revolution that can set the example for the entire world.

You are your own king or queen; be not accountable to those who wish to fulfill that role for you. Be present in every moment so that *they* are not present in your absence. You owe your country nothing except self examination and self healing. Those actions alone take care of the swirling, enumerable details that make up the rest. If a critical mass does this, it all takes care of itself. It is not time to wake up and fight; it is time to wake up and realize the fighting was the cause. We fight everyday against the inner calling; telling that voice what it speaks is impossible, while all the rational, possible has not worked.

Fight only for yourself by strengthening your mind, body, and spirit and against the fabricated obstacles in your way that seem to explain logically, yet fraudulently, that said obstacles cannot be wished away. Stare directly at the obstacle no matter the fear. Soon you will be seeing the way around or through.

There is great change coming, and many have already felt it. It is a whisper in between news snippets, well under the murmurs of the crowd. It is swelling inside the chests of all, and it will become visible. We are starting to realize where our power lies, and it is not within government, not founded and financed in the banking sector, and not attained by weaponry or military might. It is in the *I AM*, undefeatable and not for sale.

Self-Governance
VS.
Anarchy

There is no one way to govern a diverse people, but to let them govern themselves. For a person to govern him or herself, they must learn how, and this is accomplished by having the personal freedom to both triumph and fail, providing individual guideposts to discern that which is effective.

What is self-governance? Is it anarchy? No. It is the acknowledgement within that although in a seemingly limited environment of freedom, you ultimately control your personal liberty. When operating from your authentic self, you will see the keys to liberation are in your hands alone, no matter the circumstance in which you find yourself.

Yes, the land of opportunity became a land filled with opportunists. However, opportunists are people. People of all kinds will always exist. In a civilized society, rule of law is paramount. As for the structure of government, it is imperative that the law of the land be derived from a philosophy of eternal truth and not founded upon temporary, illusory structures and paradigms of the mortal ideal.

Because a government can become corrupt does not mean absence of government structure is the answer. Change in thinking does need to occur. This change needs to come from the place of original corruption—the people themselves. If the people are corrupt, their government will be corrupt. If the people forget what is eternal truth and universal law, the government will not abide by this truth, for the government is made up of people just as the society it governs.

The idea that, without government, people would not wish to dominate others, hurt others, and attain power is delusion. Self-governance is not the absence of public institutions and rule of common law. It is *not* anarchy. To think humans cannot oppress other humans without the use of public buildings and courtrooms, elections and law is absolutely ridiculous.

Our public servants are acting like "rulers". Why? This is because people allowed themselves to be ruled instead of ruling themselves. A democracy or a republic can work magnificently, but only if the people uphold their end by self-governing—doing the things themselves that they have previously refused to do. By not performing these responsibilities, the door has opened for others to do it for us. We no longer deal with each other as human beings. If we did, we would settle most of our conflicts while honoring each other even through bitter dispute. There would be more private resolution resulting in less legislation and fewer frivolous lawsuits.

As Americans, we are being ruled in the same manner as we rule our life—without appreciation of detail and faith. We make servants of food and friends and nature and expect to be treated fairly by government... Is not a government a reflection of its people?

A type of anarchy reigned in the dark ages... Not a shining example for those pushing their version of anarchy. Over and over, anarchists give the Greek origin of what anarchy means ("without rulers") and yet the Greeks never seemed to espouse anarchy in their history... So it's just a way to prove they've read a book on anarchy, the dictionary, or collectively decided to adopt a mantra; otherwise, the Greek root means nothing except that it was discussed in ancient Greece, given a term, but not applied in Greek culture. In fact, a lot of our founding philosophy came from a Greek model—anarchy was not included, but self-governance was.

Anarchists have no faith that humans could produce good leadership, yet have faith that humans could prosper in community in a purely voluntary manner. People are people, they commit terrible acts, and they commit wonderful acts. No matter the structure of government, a person can find a way to domineer their neighbor. The root of the *need* for power is the issue. Anarchists are as aware and understanding of natural law, human psychology, and how the universe truly works as "flat earthers" understand geography.

Anarchy limits human expression. In life, there are born leaders and followers. Neither of these is a human flaw, but a chance to experience life from different perspectives. Anarchy limits options for these human expressions. Government does not have to "rule" and people do not have to be slaves. These are choices of free will. One must first learn to rule himself, master himself. People do have different destinies; it is what they do with these destinies that bring forth change, good or bad.

Let us imagine life without public institutions, public servants, or law...

Someone in our imagined utopia happens to commit murder. People will want something done. There will be meetings, solutions discussed, and inevitably a repercussion rendered by the community to the offender. This seems to be what government is at its most basic.

A road needs built... People will meet, discuss, and raise funds for the road... again, it is a form of governmental action no matter how loose and carefree the process is on paper. It is still people of a community coming together to solve a basic societal issue. That is what democratic government was constructed for in the first place.

The subject of having no "rulers" is understandable. Government officials elected or not, are intended to be public servants. We have allowed them to be rulers by not ruling ourselves and letting them appear more capable than we, a group of individuals, of deciding our collective fates for us.

Often we hear the cry for our rights. This group and that group is outraged for a certain right being taken or impeded by society or its legislators. Very few are calling for responsibility. Individuals must hold inherent responsibility in such high regard as inherent right, or any structure of civil culture will topple.

Anarchists hold a cynical view of authority. Due to the corrupt nature of many in public office, they presume to view public office as a only seat of rulership. This was not the original intent of our founding, but has devolved to be such. Was it because the founding principles had changed? Did a piece of paper shuffle its words, add or subtract others, or in any way, by its own accord, become defunct or untrue? No, it was people who added to, subtracted from, and chose to interpret differently such documents.

This is a world of extremes, and we can find ourselves throwing the baby out with the bathwater when things become difficult. Soon, we feel that it was all wrong from the beginning when we find ourselves stuck in a moment of discontent. We become forgetful of times when extremes were tried and had miserably failed whether it was anarchy, collectivism, Marxism, communism, and so forth. When societies reached their pinnacle or a new age of progress such as the Renaissance, it was after a period of darkness and ruin. These great societies were filled with great individuals who contributed to the whole not by governmental force or absence of structure but by necessity breeding invention. These individuals rose to the occasion while society had crumbled around them.

There needs to be balance. The debate has become fraudulently narrowed to two choices: Do you want companies and markets to control society or big government to control society? Likeminded people will always come together to bolster their cause. The same would happen under anarchy. Each current political party touts the supremacy of their platform by reducing their opponents to the worst extremes of their platform. I contend that our republic can work, given that the people of this republic regain their authenticity. All philosophies can contribute to a proper solution in any area of need. Political parties are fine, but not for the seeking of total control of the status quo. In a world of uncertainty, it might be a tough pill to swallow, but there exists no party that is the "good guy" or "bad guy". Parties, like people, are not infallible.

To say that government or a system or a person is the sole problem is delusion. Great individuals and leaders of progress have blossomed in all eras under various societal circumstances. The bitter truth is—there is no decent excuse for failure. Anyone anywhere can rise above circumstance. To deny this is to think of human beings as less than what they truly are. In this case, all parties and ideologies have failed, for degrading the human essence is our greatest negligence.

Take a Breath

Honking horns and endless chatter, smog and fog in the mind and in the air, headaches, dizziness, cancerous cells and toxic moments all merging into a global migraine... Anxiety mounts at home and work—turn on the TV and watch stories of those who have popped from the unreleased pressure, thinking there is no respite, finally giving in to the falsehood of an uncontrollable destruction of peace.

We pile on more, hoping for the next fad to be the remedy. "If I could just..." "If this would occur..." Busy schedules grow busier, cramming in events that merely take our mind from the suffocation; instead of removing the plastic bag from around our face, we add another, tighter one.

Imagine celebrating, instead of another lackluster bank holiday or hectic holiday season that provides no chance for calm introspection, a day for a collective breath—a giant exhale for all mankind, celebrating the fact our projected concerns are not that grave and no more than manufactured hopelessness. Realizing the fabricated nature of our stress will allow us to breathe deeply, filling our lungs with the good air of inspiration and wisdom while exhaling all that does not serve us—fear doubt, anger and disillusionment.

When wrapped in a world of uncontrollable chaos, it is time to do the simplest thing we can control no matter the level of enlightenment. We breathe automatically, despite all that ails. Let us take conscious control of that breath, fill up with new air and let go of the tension… All of our shoulders relax and necks stop snapping to and fro in constant, concerned reaction… The spine settles in to its proper place, and feet step softly and surely while soaking up the strength beneath each footprint…Our heads will decompress; our eyes will see more clearly. Our hearts lighter, no longer constricted by the short choppy breaths of yesterday's turmoil, will finally let love in and compassion flow, for others and most importantly, for ourselves.

Take a breath, world. That which makes you heavy in your doings is not worth the doing. Remove the unnecessary burdens and take time to breathe and be. You are complete without crossing every item from the day's list. You are whole and there is no struggle outside of the one you have created; if you take time to breathe, there will be less time to create more anxiety, more work, and the empty timeslots on the calendar will not appear as a void to fill, rather a time already filled with bliss and satisfaction.

"God is a comedian playing to an audience that is too afraid to laugh."
—Voltaire

Take that breath. Oh how we have grown cold and hardened, too stiff to see the humor in life and revel in our stumbles, and our silliness.

We have allowed a dark paradigm to set in motion a daily routine of "stuff" we *must* do, people we *have* to love, and places we clutch with whitened knuckles, holding on so seriously we forget how they make us feel.

You have no obligation except to be, and that happens naturally. How can we be so serious when thrust into a world of continual contradiction? Your very existence is contradictory… a miracle.

There was nothing; then there was something, and not one of us can remember when there was nothing. Existence was created through contradiction, yet we aggrandize every rule and law of the universe as if it will bite our head off if we misspeak, overlook, or fall short of expectation.

Expectation is the murderer of possibility, stabbing it with *have to be's* and *should haves* and burying it in the woods next to unbiased hope. Let go and experience. Experience all you come across with the eyes of a child, consumed in awe and delighted by nuance. Laugh at the irony, giggle at your blunders and know that everyone trips over their own shoelaces; some just do it while no one happens to be watching.

Most only see amazing achievement at its completion. We may not have witnessed Thomas Edison zapping himself with electricity while he experimented with circuitry; we just know the light bulb.

To experience life at its fullest, one must learn the art of the unforced smile, even in the darkest times, knowing there has to be a punch line coming.

"Be kind, for everyone you meet is fighting a hard battle."
—Socrates

Life in this skin is not easy, but there is hope in that; it proves there is indeed a grand lesson. Somehow as we watch and interact with others, we forget they have their own story unfolding, one that brings them both enlightenment and confusion, both interchanging moment by moment.

We look at someone's past, forgetting our own learning curve. We look at someone in their present and assume they have come as far as they can, immediately judging their future as though we are steering them toward it and they have no choice but to maintain the current path.

It does not matter if you like someone, what they portray, or in what they engage... they might not like you either. We are all writing and living our own stories. We chose a certain set of obstacles and experiences, and it is no one's business as to the goings-on of them or how we navigate toward our final page.

Judgment of these battles within others dishonors our own plight. It consumes us with prejudices and excuses for intolerance. One acts, lives, chooses, or is born into a different culture, belief, or lifestyle and for whatever reason, there are those that feel it places some burden on them even if they are not living those choices or situations themselves. This is the epitome of narcissism, nurturing a catalyst for conformity, and if conformity is rigidly espoused, subtly or overtly under any number of false nomenclatures, it inevitably ends in those refusing it, and devolves into confusion, hatred, and even travesties against human rights.

If you have never struggled, you've never truly embraced living. If you have never done or been something to which at least one person is adverse, you are not fulfilling your potential to be human.

Let us reflect on all of those who may walk a different path, from a different race, a different way of being, and let us reflect upon the questions we all have concerning this unexplained life. Merging the two, we will find no reason to treat anyone with anything other than love, respect, and honor; for these are the truest values from within and we all have these in common.

Freedom for One is Freedom for All...

We can fight for freedom, but that constitutes our freedom being in someone else's grasp, causing need for us to take it back, or gain it for the first time. Where does freedom originate? At 16, we start to drive which seems to allow us a new or more freedom in our lives, yet until we came to an age where we desired this freedom, we had already felt free. Why?

As children, we are unbridled in our imagination, traveling to distant, magical lands, interacting with mythical beings and playing the hero, or any role that brought us entertainment or fulfillment.

What had changed? Did we outgrow our imaginations or did we choose not to form new purpose for imagination?

We are programmed to fight for freedom; that is like fighting to keep our blood flowing through our veins. We have freedom inherently. It is our spirit. It is our imagination.

No empire has to crumble; no city has to be overrun to oust a dictator. We are our own tyrant, dictating when it is appropriate to feel free or to feel constraint

He that is slow to anger is better than the mighty;
and he that ruleth his spirit than he that taketh a city.
—Proverbs 16:32

Grab onto your spirit and exact it into all you venture. This is your point of unencumbered freedom. This is the genesis of your creation.

Abundance springs from that place where mind, body, and soul merge. This is the place where ideas form, escape from oppression and poverty is at hand, and strength to perform the do's and pass by the don'ts exists. This is the Kingdom of God where each one of us is royalty, and we alone hold the keys to our own imagined prison cell. This is where the heart is free. This is where the million dollar idea pushes up through the dirt, blossoming into a tree of life, letting its leaves sway freely, ushering in a new perspective, a new hope, and a new dream. This is where we must recluse to heal ourselves; this is what we need to exude in order to heal our world.

If we exude only this, no darkness or tyranny will have room to fit among us. If we emit only love and light, that is all we shall see; that is all we will feel and experience. It is that simple. Are we through making it complex?

The Story of You

"Once you make a decision, the universe conspires to make it happen."
—Ralph Waldo Emerson

Your biggest weapon in defeating your mind and the maze it has concocted is this; you are unconditionally loved and supported in good times and in bad. You have had bad days, ranging from terrible to unspeakable. You have had grand days, beautiful and serene, even if the middle of clamor.

Your worst thought or deed has been forgiven. In fact, in the end of ends, no judgment ever had existed birthing need of forgiveness. You judge only yourself, if you wish. You have permission to live as your heart leads. There is no scorecard and leader board in the sky. Merely have that conversation, no matter your custom or creed. Look within and know *it* is there. Look around and witness it expressed, exactly for how it is, good, bad, or indifferent.

These are the keys of life and liberty. These are in the safety of your hands alone. Make that decision and see it all come together, wrapping around you, jostling even just for a bit, as any shifting comes with the heavy winds of change, and to completely know calm water is to have felt a typhoon.

Your spirit waits anxiously for you to discover and grab on to your story, bringing it to life with every breath you inhale, and exhaling creation, moment by moment. This is how the universe expands. Thought and expression spark new possibilities. This is what brings change from within, for if you follow your own story, your spirit will manifest through you, healing old wounds and making you whole. The spirit will conquer the mind and glow brighter than before. This will have a drastic effect on the world around you, and being will become effortless.

The pressure is removed, and it is okay to fall on your face. Relax and laugh at yourself constantly. Those that feel judged every moment of every day take a pummeling over time equal to that of a seasoned prizefighter; they endure an internal pounding to the heart. Every decision becomes hazy, squinting through a fog of other voices and memories corrupting the ability to feel one's own heart. One of the longest, heaviest chains we impose on ourselves is that of impending judgment from God, our family, our friends, and random, nameless people we pass along the way that we never see again. When this pressure is removed, for it presses upon the ego, we can start to see the decisions with clarity, as we are now seeing from the heart.

And when you do make that decision with intent and passion, it will be done. Trust that whatever comes is meant to come, and in it provides a way and an experience worth exploring, benefiting you, in turn benefiting others. Bliss is infectious. Positive mindsets will only gravitate toward likeminded beings. The same is true for the negative.

Drop the fear of judgment, of failure, of low self worth and you will experience how swiftly wisdom comes and love flows through you and outward, without effort, involuntarily. No need for crusade or public service announcement; simply being will show the example to all who wish to see it. And whoever chooses another path, that's fine too. That is their story, and they are absolutely entitled to it.

You choose how you wish to experience every day. Realize that you are in control. You can create an entirely different circumstance in an instant, no matter where you stand, sit, or run. Set it into motion, and you will have a universal force of love to see you through.

What makes you tick?
What do you love?
What brings you pain, regret, sadness?
What have you overcome?
What has left you feeling defeated?

Find your strengths and weaknesses. Behind each glaring weakness is a shining strength waiting to burst through beneath the hazy cloud of a lesson. Look for the origin of emotion, there's purpose in it. These things will help you uncover your story.

Everyone has a story. You wrote it before coming here and now you are bringing it to life. There are tragedies and comedies, love stories and mysteries, adventures and real snoozers… and sometimes we live them all in one. This life is but many lives woven together.

See what those twists and turns have revealed to you. Examine the story that has already unfolded, and what you wish to come of it. Look within to know yourself—the self that is apart from all your entwinements. Who are you? What makes you happy?

Of all the existential questions that could be posed, why are these the most overlooked? Have we gotten so outside of ourselves looking for solutions that we no longer consistently ask these to our self? Honoring these things about and within you will assist you in creating the rest of your story.

In any tale, movie, novel, or biography that ever held your attention, gripped you in a page-turning frenzy, or made you feel deeply and enlightened you to your own situations, there existed rich experiences full of joy, sadness, frustration, fear, drama, adventure, intrigue and a triumphant overcoming. These too, are your story, if you take that important step back to see it, you then can direct as well as be the lead role.

> *"To be yourself in a world that is constantly trying to make you something else is the greatest accomplishment."*
> —*Ralph Waldo Emerson*

You must first know yourself. Then own it… all of it; the parts that make you want to boast and the parts that make you ill. Face it, then dive deeper, past the blurry *could haves* and *might be's* and continuing on to the true self. That true self is unique and an expression of divinity that is yours to keep. It never parts from you, and it will never be stolen. You can give it up on your own accord, choosing to fall asleep and going on auto-pilot.

Or you can discover the power of creation within and utilize your passions in a way to develop a healing process for yourself. In these passions, your story waits for you to bring it to life. It will be different than your neighbor or friends or family. Let that individuality shine. Know that the status quo exists, but be weary of it; it changes swiftly and quietly, and soon you may be dropped or elevated at the whimsy of shifting thought.

You are the constant in every moment of your existence. Just be that, for every moment of your existence. Be you.

DECLARATION OF SELF INDEPENDENCE

When in the course of human events it becomes necessary for a person to dissolve the political bands which have connected them with another in order to seek the light within that has been encumbered by the mounting storm of misguided groupthink that inhibits the empowerment of individuality and its proper place to flourish, separate from, but connected fruitfully to the whole, the person must proclaim independence from such infringements they have allowed to infiltrate their own well being.

For such independence to be manifest, each person must hold only themselves accountable to self evaluation while accepting the onus of having bequeathed one's independence to an external source from the onset. Once ownership of the truth that we have chosen to give away our empowerment, we may then reclaim that which is solely ours and see a truly cohesive union of individuals, all expressing uniquely and harmoniously, free from past oppression and making impossible the reemergence of it in the future.

We hold that these truths are evident within the self, that all men are created equal, and all have been endowed by their creator with certain unalienable rights springing forth from within, that among these are life, liberty, and the pursuit of happiness—to secure these rights, we look not to a government instituted by other men, deriving its power from external means of propriety, but to one of self-governance by which all men seek and abide by the power within.

Whenever any form of government becomes destructive to these ends, it is the right of the individual to alter or abolish it by instituting a new way of seeing the ordinance and applications of natural law to oneself based upon the foundation of principles that lie within one's own heart, organizing the self in such form that no group of men or individual can impede upon their safety and happiness.

When an organization of officials seek to enumerate abstract individualities into finite, redundant laws, it has overstepped its purpose and usefulness, thus standing in direct opposition of the freedom of all separate individuals in vain attempt to monitor the collective, nudging them into a preconceived, generic structure of false precepts.

This has resulted in an inevitable long train of abuses and usurpations either unintended or malicious, whereby whatever the motive, the free person is transgressed and hindered. It is our right as an individual to shrug off such government and social paradigms to provide ourselves as the guards of our own security.

For this proclamation of freedom from such an environment, we must actualize certain truths from within ourselves and our own perceptions of the status of our physical surroundings, in that we only see what we have chosen to see, and allow only the taking of power what we have been willing to forgo. These transgressions we see in our world structure come only from the broken connection to our Self, made manifest into our own fears ruling over us. This must be accepted foremost; otherwise these and proceeding claims will fall short of providing such freedom and reclamation of personal pursuits.

I acknowledge that in order for this new self-governance, I, the individual of the whole, must pursue only what lies within my own heart, with compassion and love toward others that are self-ruling participants of a land.

In that, I break away from the constraints of fear mongering and doomsday exploitations, seeking the truest state of freedom that is provided by God whether or not a federal, state, or local government exemplifies these truths.

I will fear no imposition by any group of legislators, judges, administrations, or enforcements of which, knowing that I alone can read the text of my own story, and no amount of doubt-provocation or externalized seeking of power can accumulate around me with enough force to debase the undeniable truth residing within.

I will be guided and guarded by these truths and by no other man's persuasive concept of them, accepting they might be their own truths and forgiving their right to bear such ideals, for it is of no consequence to myself.

I claim independence for my own self, acting in accordance to the divine within, letting groupthink and pressures not deter me from my own pursuit of happiness, for my story is not tied to political party or the perceived struggle of a populous, instead tethered only with God and the harmonic universe abounding, wherein my true nature and freedom of spirit thrives and echoes to all generations, eternally.

Do as you will governmental bodies; it surely has no consequence to my being. Your only power has been derived by the mass misconception that you, by highest authority, hold the power and duty to allocate rights to the people. This is a wild distortion of the drafts constructed by our forefathers.

I acknowledge only, as originally intended, those rights inherent and complete within my soul and have no need for an external body to decide which right or rights to allow, no matter social trends or exaggerated illnesses of society.

I am not reflection of society, but society shall be a reflection of what I perceive of it. The change is within. The peace is within. The power is within, and I allow no other person, upon a throne, behind a podium, or in a closed-door negotiation to dictate whereby I draw my own conclusions or exact my pursuit of happiness.

I disregard the prospect and notion of impending tyranny, for I know that even threat or incarceration can not trap or squelch the spirit. The spirit is undefeatable, and in the spirit is where I reside in a place without border, without limitation, without corruption. Rather it is a place abundant with love, hope, and all the security any being requires in which to properly navigate one's journey.

Understanding that if all avow to righteous self-governance derived through peaceable, silent self-work and reflection, all will be a shining example of freedom and the result of such will be the peaceful dissolution of the contrived bonds that have disillusioned a free people.

Only by these means will arrive a sustaining union of peace that covers the land, providing this and all future generations with security and, without infringement or imposition, a way of life that will connect us with greater recognition of our fine nation and its divine worth.

www.ingramcontent.com/pod-product-compliance
Lightning Source LLC
Chambersburg PA
CBHW070358290526
45790CB00004B/1547